VGM Careers for You Series

# CAREERS FOR

# FILM BUFFS

## & Other Hollywood Types

### JAQ GREENSPON

**SECOND EDITION**

### *VGM Career Books*

Chicago  New York  San Francisco  Lisbon  London  Madrid  Mexico City
Milan  New Delhi  San Juan  Seoul  Singapore  Sydney  Toronto

Library of Congress Cataloging-in-Publication Data

Greenspon, Jaq.
    Careers for film buffs & other Hollywood types / Jaq Greenspon.— 2nd ed.
       p.   cm.  —  (Careers for you series)
       ISBN 0-07-140574-7 (pbk.)
       1. Motion pictures—Vocational guidance—United States.    2. Motion
pictures—Production and direction—Vocational guidance—United States.
3. Motion picture industry—Employees—Job descriptions—United States.
I. Title.    II. VGM careers for you series.

PN1995.9.P75G68   2003
791.43′02′93—dc21                   2002192412

· · · · · · · · · · · · · · · · · · · · · · · · · · · · · · · ·

*For Mom and Dad, Howard and*
*Ricki Greenspon: see, I told you*
*it was a real job*

1 2 3 4 5 6 7 8 9 0   LBM/LBM   2 1 0 9 8 7 6 5 4 3

ISBN 0-07-140574-7

This book is printed on acid-free paper.

# Contents

# Acknowledgments

S pecial thanks to Jane Loughman, Aren Buchanan, Faye Fulton and the kids, Don Loughman, Willie Etra, Kevin Troy Darling, Pete Dillard, Brian "Crash" Carlucci, Denise Betts, Doug J. Kerzner, Maria Rodriguez, Shea Butler, Kevin Hopps, Carol Buchanan, Sandy Mullally, Kristie Randall, Kim Christiernsson, Heidi Trotter, and the entire 2120 gang (they know who they are).

Thanks also to all the talented people in the film industry who graciously donated their time to make this project a success:

Adria Later, Studio Teacher/Welfare Worker/Baby Wrangler
Alice M. Hart, Food Stylist, Food for Film Stylists
Ambrose Ren, Researcher
Anastacia Moser, Script Supervisor
Andrew J. Zoeller, Editor, Kolbeco Productions
Anthony Sepulveda, Casting Director
Avi Kipper, Scoring Mixer
Becca Levinson, Second Assistant Director
Bill Barretta, Suit Performer
Brent Boates, Visual Effects Art Director
Carol Wyatt, "Simpsons" Animation Colorist/Color Designer
Cynthia McArthur, Fight Choreographer
Dan Persons, Film Journalist
Dan Povenmire, "Simpsons" Animator
David Barrington Holt, Creative Supervisor
David M. Jones, Model Shop Supervisor
David McGuire, Property Custodian
Frank Leasure, Prop Maker/Construction Coordinator

Gene Glick, Gaffer
Georgia Durante, Precision/Stunt Driver, Performance Two
Holly Willis, Film Teacher
Howard Parkins, "Simpsons" Animation Assistant Director
Jeff "Swampy" Marsh, "Simpsons" Animation Backgrounds
Jeffrey Allen Lynch, "Simpsons" Animation Director
Jennie Wanniski, Special Effects Fabricator
Jennifer D'Angelo, Set Dresser
John Roesch, Foley Artist, Warner Bros. Studio
Kevin Clash, Puppeteer
Kevin Holden, Production Coordinator
Kirk Thatcher, Producer/Creature Designer
Marc Spiegel, Location Manager/Scout
Marie Pfieffer, Still Photographer
Mark Phillips, Assistant Prop Master
Martin Dunn, Digitizer
Mary Jo Lang, Foley Mixer, Warner Bros. Studio
Matt Bordofsky, First Assistant Director
Patrick Moraz, Composer
Pete Michels, "Simpsons" Animation Timer
Rick Canelli, Recordist, Warner Bros. Studio
Robert Bennett, Stand-In
Robert E. Collins, Director of Photography
"Skids" Poppe, Driver
Steve Whitmire, Puppeteer
Susan Nininger, Costume Designer
William "Billy" Thomasson, Makeup Artist

# CHAPTER ONE

# So You Want to Be in Pictures

E very one of us has experienced a little bit of magic recently. It started innocently enough, when we walked into the theater and the lights went down. Then, for two hours we sat transfixed as we watched thousands of tiny images flicker past our eyes to form fluid pictures. Magic. For most of us, the magic ended at the same time the film did, when the long list of names started scrolling up the screen and the lights came back on. Not many of us read the names of the people who gave us the magic, primarily because we don't know what it is they do. We don't know what a gaffer is. We have no idea what his or her contribution to the film has to do with the final product. We don't know how we can become part of the magic.

Not knowing doesn't stop all of us, however. Every day, thousands of people arrive in Los Angeles wanting to be part of the magic, part of the film industry. Ask any ten people walking down a street in Hollywood about their screenplay, and at least nine will tell you it's coming along nicely, but what they really want to do is direct. Or act. Or produce. And while that's all well and good, not everybody can be an actor or a writer or a director or a producer. Some of us have to be the ones who make the magic in less visible ways. That's where this book comes in.

The aim of this book is to help you discover the job in the film industry that suits you best—and inspire you to go do it. Or you may just learn something you didn't know and will soon be the life of the party and the recognized movie expert among your friends and family.

The industry we're going to be talking about is built around having fun. Sure, there are long hours (the typical film set day ranges between twelve and fourteen hours, sometimes longer) and short weekends (a lot of low-budget films shoot six days a week), but ask anybody involved and he or she will tell you, "You've got to love this business before you get in; you've got to love it to stay in." If you do, too, maybe you'll come out and share the magic of yourself with the rest of the world.

In the film industry there is a mythical budgetary line that divides the "creative talent" from the rest of the crew. Your job and salary on a film are defined by whether you are above or below the line. The above-the-line people are the fearsome four—actor, writer, director, producer. Below the line is where you find the masses of people who actually bring a film together, the ones who put in the long hours, the sweat, and, yes, the magic. Theirs are the fields you can break into because anything you do now can be done somewhere in the industry.

## Stages of Production

There are four sequential sections to any type of production, be it film, television, or music video: preproduction, production, post-production, and promotion. For simplicity, the term *film* can also cover TV or music video production, unless stated otherwise.

### Preproduction

This is where the film is first conceived and prepared. The actors are hired, the set is built, the costumes are designed. Here the magic begins.

### Production

Now we're ready to start filming. Everything is prepared, and the production crew is hired. These are grips and gaffers, sound and camera crews, and more. Production gathers all the parts of the film together, including the actors' performances, and commits it all to film, continuing the magic.

## Postproduction

Here all the parts are assembled into the final film. The special effects and sound track are added, the best scenes are edited together in the correct order, and the titles are added. Eventually all that's left is the full-length feature, ready to be shown at a movie theater near you.

## Promotion

You've read the ad. You've watched the trailers. You've seen and heard and read the stars talking about their latest project. Now see the film! Promotion and publicity make sure the audience members know what it is they're supposed to spend their hard-earned money on Friday night at the local multiplex. Promotion's job is to let you know who's in the film and what it's about in order to make it the must-see of the season.

······················································

# Preview of Coming Attractions

The only problem with dividing the entire film industry into these four categories is that the various jobs tend to overlap a great deal. Therefore, with the intent of providing clarity and demystification, this book has been arranged by departments. In other words, we'll tell you what they do as opposed to when they do it. Each chapter will cover a different department.

## Production: Making the Trains Run on Time

As far as below-the-line talent is concerned, members of the production staff are the hardest-working people in showbiz. In this department, you'll find the assistant directors and the unit production managers conferring with production coordinators and location scouts. Of course, the busiest people in the office are the production assistants, or PAs, as they're so popularly known. PA is *the* entry-level job in production. From here, you can only go up: up to get the coffee, up to get an actor, up to wash the dishes, up to—you get the picture.

## Camera and Sound: The Gift of Vision and Voice

The most important thing about a movie is that you can see it. It's already dark in the theater, so if it's dark on the screen as well, the camera crew hasn't done its job properly. Likewise, the audience needs to hear what the actors are saying or the story doesn't make any sense. And if there's no dialogue, we need a dynamic sound track to enhance the drama. These are the responsibilities of the camera and sound departments.

## Grip and Electric: A Light Touch

Are you good with your hands? Do you like setting things up and taking them down a few hours later when you've got the shot? Or do you like playing with electricity? Either way, you belong with the grip and electric department. These are the men and women who set up the lights, run the cables, and move the heavy stuff. This is also where you'll discover the meaning of those elusive job titles, *gaffer* and *best boy.*

## Art: Setting the Scene

This is the art department, but don't let the title fool you. The category is broad, and many things qualify. In fact, *anything* seen on the screen was created or approved by members of the art department. If you can hold a paintbrush, there's work for you here.

## Makeup and Costumes: Looking the Part

No matter what the actors look like by the time their images make it to the screen, they have made a trip to the makeup and wardrobe trailer before they got there. Even if the scene requires two actors to look as if they have just gotten out of bed in the morning, a hairstylist has to neatly arrange their hair in a disorderly fashion, a makeup artist has to create the perfect look of "sleepy and yet refreshed," and sleepwear must be carefully picked out or designed to complement the hair and makeup work. All in all, if you've got fashion sense, somebody might put you to work here.

## Animation: Drawing on Your Imagination

Welcome to the specialized world of animation. This is where you'll find out how two-dimensional drawings are made to look three-dimensional and alive. After reading this chapter, you'll have a whole new respect for the people who have been bringing you cartoon entertainment for so many years.

## Special Effects: Lifelike . . . Only More So

How many times have we imagined being on a distant planet, fighting aliens alongside the crew of our spaceship, our lasers blasting holes in the walls and futuristic furniture? If that's what the script calls for, then a visit the special effects department is required. This one-stop shopping can give you creatures, space-ships, lasers, and explosions. If your dreams run toward the fantastic, special effects can help you make them real.

## Editing: The Cutting Edge

One thing that separates film from other visual arts is the ability to edit. The picture editor has the power to force you to look at something you don't want to or draw your attention to something you may have missed. The sound editor does the same thing with dialogue or gunshots or alien voices. The attention to detail and patience required to be either type of editor make these professionals worth their weight in gold.

## On the Fringes

If you've gotten this far and still haven't found anything that suits your particular talents, look no further than this chapter, where most everything else done in, on, or around a film is covered. Do you know something about animals? You can be a wrangler or even a trainer. Do you have good organizational skills? There are always celebrities looking for personal assistants. Even if you don't think you have anything to offer, films are made on every topic, and your services could come in handy as a technical consultant. No matter what you do in real life, there's a job for you somewhere in the film industry.

## For Further Information

The film industry is always open to accept new people. This book will tell what the jobs are and what you need to know to do them. One of the best places to learn these skills is film school. It's not the only place, but it will give you a good opportunity to try things and get hands-on experience. Following is a list of just some of the film schools in the country. You also can check with your local college or university to find out if it offers any filmmaking courses.

American Film Institute
Center for Advanced Film Study
2021 North Western Avenue
Los Angeles, CA 90027
www.afi.com

Brooks Institute of Photography
801 Alston Road
Santa Barbara, CA 93108
www.brooks.edu

California Institute of the Arts (CalArts)
School of Film and Video
24700 McBean Parkway
Valencia, CA 91355
www.calarts.edu

Columbia University
Film Division
School of the Arts
513 Dodge Hall
2960 Broadway
New York, NY 10027
www.columbia.edu/cu/arts/film

Dartmouth College
Film Studies, Drama Department
Wilson Hall, Third Floor
Hinman Box 6194
Hanover, NH 03755
www.dartmouth.edu/~film

New York University (NYU)
Undergraduate Institute of Film and Television
721 Broadway, Tenth Floor
New York, NY 10003
www.nyu.edu/tisch/filmtv/program_ug.html

Northwestern University
Department of Radio/Television/Film
1905 Sheridan Road
Evanston, IL 60208
www.rtvf.northwestern.edu

San Francisco State University
Film and Creative Arts Interdisciplinary Department
1600 Holloway Avenue
San Francisco, CA 94132
www.sfsu.edu

School of the Art Institute of Chicago
Film, Video, and New Media
112 South Michigan Avenue, Third Floor
Chicago, IL 60603
www.artic.edu/saic/programs/depts/undergrad/fvnm.html

University of California, Los Angeles (UCLA)
Department of Film, Television, and Digital Media
405 Hilgard Avenue
Box 951361
Los Angeles, CA 90095
www.filmtv.ucla.edu/filmtv/ftvhome.htm

University of California, Los Angeles (UCLA) Extension
Entertainment Studies
10995 Le Conte Avenue
Los Angeles, CA 90024
www.uclaextension.org

University of Southern California (USC)
School of Cinema/Television
University Park
Los Angeles, CA 90007
www.usc.edu/schools/cntv

# CHAPTER TWO

# Production

## Making the Trains Run on Time

The bus stops on the corner of Hollywood and Vine, and you step out into the sunny Southern California weather. You've just arrived in Hollywood, and you're ready to start making movies. All around you are actors and writers and directors waiting to be discovered.

But that's not for you; you want to be involved with production. Ever since you were a little kid, you've been hearing that word, *production*, with all its mythic connotations, echoing through your dreams. Now you're ready to make it a reality. Where do you go, who do you see, what do you know?

More important, what can you do?

Production is the place where everything happens. The busiest places to be during a film is the production office. It is also one of the best places to be if you want to learn all you can about the filmmaking process. All the hiring, casting, and decision making are done by the people in production.

The production staff also works the longest on any given shoot. Once you start with a film in preproduction, you're stuck with it almost until it's released, unless you're working directly for the production company itself and not for the film. If that is the case, you'll be with the project until it has run its financial course. It could be years.

Where do you start? At the bottom, of course.

# Production Assistant (PA)

As the story goes, a low-budget film producer was making a movie at a local mall. When the crew members arrived, they couldn't get into the parking structure because the gate was down and the exit had spikes blocking the way with a sign: "Warning: Do not back up, severe tire damage." A guy from the art department offered to quickly build a wood ramp so all the vehicles could get over the spikes. The producer thought about it for a minute, then said, "Don't waste the lumber. Throw a PA down there; that's what they're for."

Maybe it didn't happen quite that way, but a lot of people who have been production assistants won't deny that's how they have been treated at some point in their careers. But they wouldn't trade it for anything.

The production assistants are the gofers of the film set. All departments have them. If, after you finish this book, you still haven't found which career is suited to you and you still know you want to make movies, become a production assistant. You'll get to experience all aspects of production; then all that's left is for you to pick the one you like.

As a production assistant involved in the production department (production assistants in other departments have slightly different jobs, but the feeling is the same), your responsibilities can range from making sure the star has coffee in the morning to stopping traffic on a busy intersection in the middle of rush hour so your director can get the shot. You should be prepared to help out everywhere and listen to everyone. If you stay one step ahead of what the assistant directors are doing and are there to help them before they call for you, it will eventually earn you a promotion into their ranks.

Getting a job in the entertainment industry is not based entirely on who you know, but it doesn't hurt to know a lot of people. You can meet these kinds of people by working as a production assistant and doing it well. Average pay for production assistants starts at between $50 and $100 a day—and they work for it.

## Secretary

Okay, being a secretary in the film industry isn't that far from being a secretary in any other business. The difference lies in the promotion possibilities. A good secretary in any other field is the lifeblood of the office, and maybe she or he will be promoted, but for most, it can be a career in itself. In filmmaking, volunteering for a secretary assignment can get you in the door of a production company, and from there you're poised to take any path to any career you want.

Naturally, if all you want to be is a secretary, there are better offices in which to work. To be a film secretary, you must want to work in film, and you must shine doing the grunt work. You'll function as a support staff for the producer, answering phones, organizing meetings, and generally keeping the office running. Often, you'll be credited as the producer's assistant, but what you really are is a lifeline to keep the production moving forward smoothly.

· · · · · · · · · · · · · ·

## Runner

A runner is basically an office production assistant. This person mainly waits at the production office (assuming the office is not located on the set), ready to run to the set with new script pages from the producer; or to pick up a prop, which could be anything from a baseball hat to a stuffed coyote, for the prop master; or to fetch and deliver lunch. While waiting, the runner will answer phones and, yes, make the coffee, but mainly a runner picks up and delivers anything and everything between the production office and the set.

In a lot of instances, the runner may become a production assistant once actual production starts. From there, it's only a short hop to becoming an assistant director.

## Assistant Director (AD)

Despite what the title implies, the assistant director is not like a vice president, waiting in the wings in case the director does something drastic, like die or disagree with the studio executives. The assistant director does not second-guess the director and attempt to position the camera. What the assistant director does is, literally, assist the director. Theoretically, the director must concentrate on the film as a whole, from beginning to end. The AD, then, has the responsibility of keeping everything running smoothly, enabling the director to concentrate on the artistic vision.

There are several levels in the ranks of an assistant director. Each level has its own responsibilities and disadvantages.

## Second Assistant Director

The second assistant director is the funnel for information on the set. Ask Becca Levinson, who recently performed the job for "MTV Movie Shorts" (used on its movie awards show) and the film *The Last Producer*. Becca worked her way up through the ranks, starting as a production assistant.

On a film, her job is to help the first AD implement the schedule. In this respect, she manages the set, taking care of all the day-to-day activities.

The second assistant director's day actually starts the day before. At the end of a shooting day, the second assistant director will prepare and distribute the call sheet, which is a listing of the crew, actors, scenes, locations, and call times for the following day. The call time is the time at which people are expected on the set to start work. This time can vary tremendously, depending on which scenes are being shot and when they take place. If you are shooting a night scene, then your production day may start at sundown and finish at sunrise. Schedules are created by taking the scene-by-scene breakdowns and boiling down the information for the prepared call sheet forms. Also included on the forms are the props and sets that will be "working," or used, that day and any special requirements for makeup or costuming. If you are preparing the call sheet and an actor is going to be spending four hours in makeup to get his face looking like half of it was blown off in a gunfight, everybody needs to know so they can prepare for it.

At the start of a shooting day, Becca is one of the first people on the set. Because of this, she can be working as many as seventeen or eighteen hours a day, every day, up to six days a week. And she needs to be there. She needs to answer questions and make sure things are running smoothly. As in any business, activities on a set follow a certain chain of command. When there is a question, the first person to ask is the second assistant director, who should be able to find out the answer. She cautions anyone looking to get into the field, "Beware of the hours and the commitment."

On any film produced in cooperation with unions, there will be a number of unions to deal with because each department has its own. It is Becca's job as second assistant director to keep up with the various rules and regulations of these unions to ensure the producers are aware about possible meal penalties, for example, or anything that might cause the film to go over budget.

Going over budget is something all producers are worried about. It is the assistant director's team, of which Becca is part, that attempts to keep the whole production on a safe and efficient schedule to stay within the budget.

While Becca loves what she does, it's taken her awhile to get where she is. "There are ups and downs," she says, "both emotional and financial in freelance work. You don't just walk onto a set and become an AD. The union has years of requirements you need to fulfill in order to be in the Directors Guild of America (DGA) as an AD. When you start, and even once you're in the union, there are times when you'll still need to take out the trash and fetch coffee. You'll also be keeping morale up." So you have enjoy what you're doing because, as Becca says, "it's hard to keep other people happy and motivated if you don't enjoy what you do yourself."

## Second 2nd Assistant Director or Trainee

When you read the credits at the end of the film and you see the term *DGA Trainee*, this refers to the second 2nd assistant director. The trainee will do the same job as a second 2nd AD, but the trainee has gone through the Directors Guild of America assistant director program first. A second 2nd AD will have worked up from a position as production assistant, but the two are roughly equivalent.

During a production, the trainee is learning the jobs of those above and helping to manage those below. But the trainee also has responsibilities of her or his own. The trainee must fill out most of the paperwork on the set. For example, the trainee fills out the actors' time cards and sends the reports back to the Screen Actors Guild (SAG). The daily production report also falls under the trainee's jurisdiction. This report lets the studio know exactly what happened during the day's shooting. If a piece of equipment failed and stopped production for half a day, then the production report will mention it. This report is primarily for the purposes of studio accounting. A half day's failure could cost as much as $50,000 or more, and there should be a record as to why things are behind schedule.

**The Directors Guild Training Program.** To participate in the DGA training program, you must first pass a written test designed to assess job-related skills. After passing this test, which is given once a year between February and April, you move into a series of interviews held during the late spring and into the summer. In the late summer, the final candidates are accepted into the program.

The program itself covers four hundred days of work during a two-year period. As you work through the program, you are assigned to a number of different types of guild-sanctioned productions, from big-budget TV shows to low-budget features and everything in between. At the end of each assignment, you are given a progress report by the ADs on the set. The trainee's pay scale is increased every hundred days, ranging from $521 per week for the first hundred days to $640 per week for the last. Trainees are also required to attend regularly scheduled seminars that cover a variety of topics designed to increase performance as assistant directors. In the New York program, they are also assigned for one-week stints at various ancillary tasks to give them a wider range of experience with what happens in the industry outside the film set itself.

Upon graduating from the program, the trainee becomes eligible for membership in the Directors Guild of America, available for workers within the film, television, or video industries. An informative video titled *Autographs and Sunglasses* is available from the training program website.

## First Assistant Director

This is where the fun really starts. The first assistant director is the director's right hand, the one who keeps everything moving in a generally forward direction. But the first assistant director's job doesn't start when the cameras roll. By that time, the first assistant director has been on the project for at least several weeks if not a month or more. This lead time is needed to prepare and coordinate everything that will happen during the shoot. For Matt Bordofsky (who, incidentally, got his start after reading the first edition of this book and has gone on to work on such movies as *The X-Men* and TV shows such as "EZ Streets," "Pop Stars," and "Meet the Marks"), preparing for anything now comes easy. "When I started, I immediately got in over my head as a PA," he says. While he was struggling to stay afloat, he quickly became a pillar of the production and someone people knew they could count on to keep a cool head in any situation.

Matt's first job, and one of the toughest, is making the break-downs, which are created as the first assistant director reads through the script several times, each time pulling out different information and organizing it by scene number. If the film includes a special prop, like a handheld scanner for one of the Star Trek films, for example, the first AD marks down every time that prop is mentioned in the script. The end result is a list of all the props, special costumes, locations, and other details involved in the film. Each department will also do this, but only looking for the specific things it will need to take care of. The first AD will have the only complete list. The first AD will also note which actors are in which scenes. By this time the script has been literally ripped apart. The next step is for the first assistant director to put it back together in an order designed for maximum efficiency.

This order then becomes the shooting schedule. The order is not chronological—it doesn't follow the story scene by scene. If there are three shots required in the same location, the AD will schedule them together, regardless of where they fall in the film. The same is true in scheduling actors. Actors are busy people, and if all their work can be scheduled in a block of time, they prefer it, as does the producer, especially if the actor is getting paid by the day. Matt likes to think of it this way: "Regardless of script or show, you have to treat it like it's your own—their money is your money."

Also taken into account is the scheduling of night shots so the production doesn't break any union rules. But even this schedule is not set in stone. If four days are scheduled at an exterior location and it rains during two of those days (or the director happens to be ahead of schedule), a good first assistant director will have several incidental shots set aside that can be done at any time, at any location, so the production does not come to a halt.

New script pages also can change this schedule, especially on a television show. Because of the time difference, a first assistant director may have to describe a new prop or set piece to the department building it before the department has had a chance to see the script changes. All information originates with the first assistant director, which doesn't always make him or her the most popular person on the set. This suits Matt fine. "I'm not there to make friends; I'm there to make the day."

The first assistant director works one-on-one with the director and will do whatever is possible to make the director happy. This may be anything from intercepting a problem and taking care of it to taking the director to get a hamburger and talk about what's going on. The first assistant director knows what's going on everywhere on the set and makes sure it's the way the director likes it. Matt says the best advice he ever heard on a set was "More *A*, less *D*," meaning you're there to be the assistant, not the director. It's a tough job, but somebody's got to do it. And people like Matt make all the difference.

## Assistant to the Producer or Director

Now that we've established what an assistant director does, we must talk about the functions of the assistant to the producer or director. The jobs may sound the same, but there is a slight difference—a two-word difference, to be exact: "to the." These little words provide all the distinction needed to separate the assistant to the director from the assistant director.

Being an assistant to the producer or director can mean anything from being the producer's executive secretary to being the guiding and stabilizing force in the director's life while the director is engrossed in his or her latest masterpiece. Your responsibilities can range from typing letters and making phone calls five days a week to buying the director's groceries, feeding the dogs, and staying over several nights a week to make sure the director is doing everything he or she is supposed to be doing. Granted, this may be an extreme case, but if you work as an assistant to the producer or director, you will probably be asked to do a lot more than you might think is in your job description. But the job does have its own rewards.

Very often, an assistant to the producer or director will go on to do something else, like head a production of her or his own. Kathleen Kennedy, now head of her own company and producer of such megahits as *Jurassic Park III* and *A.I.*, once worked as Steven Spielberg's assistant.

To get started as an assistant to the producer or director is both easier and harder than any of the other careers listed in this book. There really aren't any unions or job boards for the position, so finding out about it may be a bit difficult. If you do find out about it, chances are it was because someone you know told you. That person may know a famous director or producer who is looking for an assistant and recommend you. Then you're going in already recommended. This is the way most assistants to the producer or director find work, although if you watch the trade journals, you will sometimes see help-wanted ads for just these jobs.

One last thing to remember: these positions are also available for people who want to assist movie stars and even some of the better-paid and more well-known writers. These people are known as personal assistants, but the job is the same, and the possibilities for advancement are just as good. The stories are common about an actor's assistant who then went on to produce that actor's Academy Award–winning film. You never know what could happen.

## Unit Production Manager

The unit production manager functions for the producer in almost the same way the first assistant director functions for the director. In some cases, the unit production manager and the first assistant director are the same person. When the two are separate, the unit production manager will often come on to a film in time to prepare the budget and oversee the production staff. During production, he or she will keep an eye on schedules and make sure they coincide with the budget. The unit production manager acts as the producer's representative when the producer isn't on the set.

# Transportation Captain

Now that you have a crew together, how are you going to get them from place to place? What about all the production and picture vehicles? Someone has to be in charge of all this, and that person is the transportation captain.

On each production, there are a certain number of production vehicles. These are trucks and cars assigned to the various departments for their particular needs. A prop master will need a prop truck—something covered and rather large, such as a small moving van—to hold all the props. The camera department will need a truck to carry all the camera gear as well, and it must have a darkroom in which to load film into the canisters.

Every piece of equipment, from lipstick to lights, needs to fit into a vehicle. Wardrobe and makeup each need a truck to hold equipment and supplies. Sometimes, vehicles will be included in the rental package. The same place from which the production gets the camera equipment may also rent a camera truck to carry it all. A full grip package will usually include a five-ton (or larger) truck to carry all the heavy instruments as well as pull the generator. Every production also needs a couple of plain old pickups to handle the odds and ends on a day-by-day basis.

That covers the equipment, but what about the actors? The actors all need dressing rooms, and, if they're big stars, they usually require their own trailers. Transportation has to arrange for all of these, too. To handle a bunch of dressing rooms at the same time, the captain will rent something called a honey wagon, which is a large trailer already subdivided into little rooms. Each room will generally have a bed, a chair, and a little table in front of a lighted mirror. Each honey wagon will also have a set of bathrooms for the performers assigned there.

Last but not least, the transportation department must also handle the picture cars. These are the cars actually seen in the movie. If the car is valuable and needs to be carried on a flatbed truck from location to location, then the transport captain needs one more vehicle in the fleet. But once this fleet is assembled, what the captain needs more than anything else is people to drive it all from location to location.

············

## Driver

If all you are is a driver, you've got one of the easiest jobs in the industry. Ask "Skids" Poppe. He's been a driver for a number of films, and he really enjoys it. In fact, that's where he got his nickname. It seems Skids has a tendency to rely a bit heavily on the brakes and leaves a trail every time he comes screeching to a halt. "I like to let the crew know I'm there," he says. As for his job, Skids doesn't do much else besides drive. He'll bring his assigned truck to the location and park it. He then has the rest of the afternoon free to read or play video games and then be ready to move again to the next location when the director calls for it. On a union shoot, Skids, a member of the teamsters, isn't even allowed to do anything else, even if he wanted to. Not a tough job once you get it, but the preparation can be grueling. Skids has earned licenses and certificates to drive almost any type of wheeled vehicle, from a motorcycle to a city bus to a full semi with a double trailer. It took a lot of training, but Skids says he wouldn't trade his job for anything.

·····················

## Accountant

If you're a producer, you're in charge of the money. (Sure, that's a bit simplified, but it'll serve our purposes.) You can't be there every minute of every day to watch over who's spending what, so you do the next best thing: you hire an accountant to handle these matters for you. But what happens if the film has some location shots as well as studio interiors, or you've got productions running at five separate places all over town? You need to have people at each set to cover the finances. That's why you need both location and studio accountants.

The best thing about being an accountant in the film industry is that you do the same thing you'd do if you were an accountant in any other company. It's one of the rare crossover jobs. Sure, you should know about film costs and how to read a budget, but working as an intern or an assistant can teach you that. The primary difference between a studio and a location accountant is the amount of suntan lotion needed on the job. A location accountant will keep an eye on the budget and schedule and report it all back to the studio. The studio accountant will then take the data from the set and put all of it into the overall production reports. It's a lot of numbers, and the people who are good at it run Hollywood.

. . . . . . . . . . . . . . . . . . . . . . . . . . . . . .

# Casting Director

A star is born. No, not the movie. The real-life job of the casting director is to make stars—or more specifically, to give actors work.

Anthony Sepulveda is responsible for casting all the speaking roles for many of Warner Bros. Television's hit shows, such as "The West Wing" and "Friends." Anyone wanting to play a part, from a guest star to the third man in the alley, must first pass through Anthony's office.

It goes like this: When the script comes in, Anthony reads it and then sends a copy to a company called Breakdowns, which breaks down the script into two parts. The first is a small paragraph about each character, and the second is a speech and line count. These are then sent to agents, who use the information to gauge what kinds of actors will be appropriate for the parts.

The agents then send out photos and resumes to the casting director. Anthony receives hundreds of photos for each role advertised and narrows the field down to twenty-five or thirty based on looks and credits alone. These few, along with actors Anthony may have seen in local theater productions or may know from past auditions, are invited to audition directly for him.

The first audition is called a prereading, and it is done solely for the casting director. Anthony weighs all the auditions and from the initial thirty or thirty-five picks five to read for himself, the producer, and the director. The final casting decisions are made together by all three. Bigger stars, with name recognition, may bypass some of this process and be asked to participate in a film or show directly by the director or producer. But even if you think you have a big name in the field, it's always wise to make sure the casting director knows who you are.

Once the roles have been cast, Anthony negotiates with each actor to work out the contract arrangements. For larger roles and leads in films, the negotiations are handled by entertainment lawyers working with the casting director.

This process is followed for each character on a feature film and all the new characters each week for series television. (Regular cast members for TV series have contracts negotiated before the season starts that cover all the episodes for that season.)

What makes a casting director good is having the ability to think creatively—for example, doing things such as casting against type (if an actor always plays a villain, casting him as the hero is against type) or seeing something different in the part and presenting the director with several options. A good memory also comes in handy. Being able to recall a good performance from the movie you saw two years ago and then bringing the actor in when the time is right is very helpful. Anthony goes to see a lot of films and as many stage plays as he can. He says the most fulfilling part of his job is discovering new talent, and he never knows where that's going to happen.

## Location Scout

If the entire movie is going to be filmed on a soundstage, then there is no need for a location scout. Most films, though, have at least one exterior location, and as long as there is one, you need someone to find the right one.

As a location scout, Marc Spiegel spent a good deal of his film career on the road, looking for just such locations. He read the script and talked to the location manager to determine which sites he was supposed to find. Then he set off, camera in hand, to find the perfect places to shoot.

A location scout relies heavily on his or her memory. Marc says that after a while, everything starts to look like a location. He would happen to notice a lovely old Victorian house, or a beautiful cliff overlooking the ocean, and file it away in the back of his mind. Later, when he read a script that called for a "nice Victorian house," he'd have the exact spot in mind.

Supposing the Victorian house became a selected location. Marc's next job was to talk to the owners of the house and find out if they'd be interested in having their home used as a film location. In this part of his job, he had to be the ultimate diplomat because he was the first representative of the production the home owners would meet. Marc then explained what the film was and how glamorous it would be to be involved.

Once the home owners were interested, Marc started taking pictures. He took panoramic shots of the entire site as well as specialized pictures of things specifically required by the script. The pictures didn't have to be perfect, just in focus and showing the location as well as can be. These were handed in or, as is becoming more and more common, E-mailed to the location manager. Then Marc was off to the next site.

When the film he was working on was shooting in California, where Marc was based, he took day trips out to see various locations, rarely staying overnight. Out of state, however, is a different matter. On the rare occasions when a production sent Marc out of town, his memory of Hollywood locations did him no good. Whenever he traveled outside the state, then, the first thing Marc did was contact the local film commission and explain to them his production's needs.

Being a location scout is a nice way to break into the industry, if you can find someone to give you a chance. Once you get hired, you'll need a couple of good cameras, both 35 mm and digital, and a reliable form of transportation to get you from location to location (you'll be reimbursed for mileage and paid a rental fee for your equipment). A rudimentary knowledge of architecture styles is mandatory. When you get sent out to find that Victorian house, you'd better know what Victorian style looks like. According to Marc, every location scout has four resources to draw from at all times: memory, friends, state film libraries, and location services. Use them all, and you'll always have the right location within reach.

## Location Manager

One step up from location scout is location manager. Often, especially on lower-budget films, the manager is also the scout. When you start as a scout, it usually won't take very long before you're filling the position of location manager. It didn't take Marc Spiegel long before he was not only finding the locations but negotiating for them as well. He's been responsible for securing sites for such films as *American History X* and *Attraction*.

The way Marc describes his current job as location manager is "someone hired by the producer to please the director." In addition, he has to be the home owners' best friend.

Once several locations have been found, whether by Marc or one of the scouts working for him, Marc goes through them all, narrowing them down to the ones he's going to present to the director. The criteria he uses to decide are not based solely on script requirements. He has to figure out the logistics in making sure the crew can work in the location. If the house is beautiful and perfect for the shot but is located on a tiny island and the only way to get there is by canoe, then there won't be any place to park the generator or the prop truck, and the location is unusable.

When Marc has picked his finalists, he'll go to the home owners and negotiate the rental price. The rental price includes a daily or weekly fee and a plan for repairing any damage done by the film crew. It also details what the home owners' involvement will be once filming starts. Most productions prefer to have the home owners staying at a hotel (paid for by the production) while filming is taking place. With the rental price and details worked out for all the possible sites, Marc shows them all to the director.

The director makes a decision, and Marc moves to the next part of his job—getting the permits and insurance to make sure the filming is legal. This is very important. The location manager is the one who can and will be arrested if the film is not carrying the proper permits, which is why you should always be nice to the people in the permit office. If you're filming outside your normal area, the local film commission will help you determine which permits are needed and how to go about getting them.

Insurance is in the same category. All states require that the production carry a certain amount of insurance (the amount varies from state to state), and it is up to the location manager to include the locations in the policy.

The day before filming starts, Marc goes over the location with an eye for preexisting damages—things like holes in walls or broken glass—that the home owner could try to blame on the crew later. On the day of filming, Marc is the first one to arrive. He greets the home owners, puts them at ease, then sends them off to the hotel. Once the trucks start arriving, Marc has already figured out where they all need to park and directs them to their spots. When everyone has arrived, Marc is finished and doesn't have to be back until the shooting day is finished, and then only to make sure things are put back the way they were. In between, he has the time to find new locations or prepare other locations for the following day.

Being a location manager is a freelance position, meaning that you are hired from shoot to shoot. Since you're not under contract, you want to do a good job so you'll get hired again. This means delivering the locations. It also means if you have a group of locations you can go back to again and again, your job will be made a lot easier. Because of the inherent diplomacy involved in location managing, Marc thinks it's the right job to teach some of the skills needed as a producer, which wouldn't be a bad promotion for someone who started out running around taking pictures.

························

## Script Supervisor

What is the worst job on the set? According to Anastacia Moser, it's script supervisor. Why? "Everyone hates you," she says. The reason everyone hates you is because part of your job is making sure everyone else does theirs. Script supervisors, also known by the title *continuity*, make sure the shots match. Since a film is not shot in sequence, a scene inside a building may be shot on the first day of filming, and the scene showing the actors walking into the building could be shot on the last day. Three months or more may pass between those two events, and it's the script supervisor's job to see that the hair, makeup, and costumes all match in those two scenes.

The script supervisor can start work as late as the day before principal photography starts. Anastacia needs the one day to set up her script for work, and then she's ready to go. To set up her script, Anastacia puts it in a three-ring binder and marks off shots. The back of the previous script page, also divided by shot, serves as a place for notes. Anastacia thus has a full page to write on in addition to the actual script page, and she'll use all of it before a shot is over.

Anastacia writes down what each character looks like as well as any specific props and set dressings that are important to the scene. Polaroids are taken of each scene, either by the script supervisor or the various departments for visual records to go along with written notes. For even greater detail, Anastacia makes notes on each individual take. (A "take" happens each time the camera rolls film. Some scenes can have as many as one hundred takes before the director feels the actors have given the desired performance.) She notes the exact length of the scene, which film reel and sound tape it's on, and a description of the shot. If the shot is over the shoulder, shot with a 50 mm lens on a dolly with a crane, that all goes into the record. As a continuity person, you can never have too many notes. Anastacia's advice: "If the director says it, note it down."

The main reason for making so many notes comes after the cameras have stopped rolling. The director relies heavily on the script supervisor during postproduction and editing, and all those notes can come in handy when the director is looking for a specific take.

A prime example of a bad continuity job is the courtroom scene in *Jagged Edge,* in which the character, played by Glenn Close, wears three different outfits during the space of one day in court. Another place to watch for continuity breaks is in the length of a cigarette ash or the level of a drink in a glass.

Anastacia suggests not even attempting script supervision unless you are extremely detail oriented and work well under pressure. If that doesn't scare you, grab your stopwatch and jump right in.

## Production Coordinator

Kevin Holden is a production coordinator. In film terms, this means he has the most contact with the outside world. The equivalent job in real life would be dispatcher. Kevin oversees the entire production from the office. Almost all paperwork generated by the production comes from his desk, and he has to keep track of it all.

When he's hired (about eight weeks before principal photography), Kevin starts by arranging things, such as renting the office equipment he needs to do his job. He coordinates all the permits the location people are getting and files them, keeping them accessible.

He works with the various department heads, making sure they have everything they need and arranging for it if they don't. This could be anything from having enough Polaroid film to last for the duration of filming (it's bought by the crate) to getting grip tape in the right colors. If Kevin himself isn't getting the supplies, then he's handing out the purchase orders for them.

When the production has to travel out of town, the production coordinator has to make the arrangements. If an actor is flying in and needs to be picked up at the airport in a limousine, Kevin is the one calling the limo companies to get the best price. His job consists of a lot of phoning, faxing, typing, and filing, as well as being able to fill requests for anything at any time. The way crew members usually start conversations with the production coordinator is, "I need . . ."

During production, the coordinator works longer than the running crew. Kevin has to be in before the crew to make sure everything is ready for the day's work and can't leave until well past the time he's passed out the call sheet for the next day's schedule. It's not the easiest job on the set, and the consolation is that if you're doing it well, nobody will notice you are doing it at all.

## Playback Technician

Whenever you're watching a film and you see a television screen showing something, you know playback has been there. Playback is responsible for any video images seen on film. Since film shoots at twenty-four frames per second and video shoots at thirty frames per second, they don't match up. The playback technicians have to make it match so you don't get video roll, which is a distracting vertical roll in the picture.

Playback also puts down any graphics seen on the screen, such as in a news story scene. If the newscasters' names are written across the bottom of the scene, playback put them there.

## Researcher

The next time you don't know the answer to a rather perplexing question, try calling your local library and asking the staff at the reference desk. They should, with a minimum of trouble, be able to answer your question. If you're a researcher, you are the one who gets to call the library.

Your job is one of knowing things. If you're good at Trivial Pursuit and you like reading the encyclopedia for fun, you have definitely found your niche. That's what happened to Ambrose Ren. He knew something someone else wanted to know, and suddenly he was doing research for a writer. "I got a call one day asking me what year some old film was made, and I told the guy. It seems he was working on a screenplay about old-time actors and got my name from a friend who told him I knew all about this stuff."

Ambrose went from just answering questions about old movies to the writer's next project, which had to do with combat pilots, something he didn't know anything about. (If you ask him now, though, Ambrose could tell you more than you'd care to know about the F-4 Phantom, used extensively in Vietnam.)

"My job is finding out information for the writer, so all he has to do is ask, and I should be able to answer—or at least be able to find the answer quickly," Ambrose says.

In addition to gathering information, researchers can also be used to track down photographs or historical documents. Sometimes a director will need to know what the number one song was for a certain week of the year the film takes place so the main character can be singing it. The researcher must then not only find out the song but also find the words and possibly even be able to locate a copy of the single to be used in the shot. Today, with the Internet, this is much easier than it used to be. Websites and information services such as iNetNow.com may make your life easier, but knowing where to look for information is still part of the job description.

Not all researchers work for writers or for specific films. There are some research agencies that specialize in certain information. The ability and desire to learn is the best asset you can bring to this detail-oriented job.

## For Further Information

The wheels of any film production move under the command of the production team. Like a sergeant in a battle, a film's schedule and budget can be made or broken by the team working on it. The following organization and books can help you find out how to become a member of the team.

Assistant Directors Training Program
Directors Guild of America
14724 Ventura Boulevard, Suite 775
Sherman Oaks, CA 91403
www.dgptp.org

### Books

Alves, Jeff. *How to Break into the Film Business: The Production Assistant Handbook*. Studio City, CA: Players Press.

Horwin, Michael. *Careers in Film and Video Production*. Burlington, MA: Focal Press, Elsevier Science/Harcourt.

Konigsber, Ira. *The Complete Film Dictionary*. New York: Penguin.

Sevilla, C. R., and Shirley Ulmer. *The Role of the Script Supervisor in Film and Television*. Fern Park, FL: Hastings House Book Publishers.

Silver, Alain, and Elizabeth Ward. *The Film Directors Team*. Lake View, NY: Silman-James Press.

# CHAPTER THREE

# Camera and Sound

## The Gift of Vision and Voice

The scene is set: A candlelight dinner for two. Watching, you can almost make out the napkins artfully arranged on the two plates sitting across from each other, resting on a tablecloth of an indeterminate color. The silverware glints brightly, obscuring any detail as to pattern. In the background, an original piece of music plays, distorting badly as it tries to fill the space of the scene. The lovers enter and take their seats. Their faces are cut in half by the top of the screen so only their lips and noses show. They whisper to one another in hushed tones. You think he is telling her how in love he is. Or he could be breaking it off, you're not sure. The couple in front of you isn't sure, either, and the old man leans to his wife and asks, rather loudly, the question you have been dying to ask: "What did he say?"

What's wrong with this picture?

Everything. If you ever see this type of scene, the camera and sound crews haven't done their jobs well. But unless you're watching one of those commercials where the camera is constantly moving and you're never quite sure of the product being advertised, you'll rarely see or hear such bad problems in a professional production.

Film is a unique medium in that it can force you to look at something, even if you don't want to, and it can clarify or distort what you hear to provide dramatic tension or comedic relief. This manipulation falls to the camera and sound departments, which have the responsibility of making sure you can see and hear everything the director wants you to see and hear.

Let's start with members of the camera crew.

## Director of Photography

The director of any film has enough to handle just dealing with the actors and the story being told. The one thing the director does not want to have to worry about is the technical crew. That's where the director of photography (DP), also called cameraman (even if the DP is a woman), comes in to play. The DP's job is to help the director tell the story using every tool available. Since film is primarily a visual medium, the main tool used is the camera.

Robert E. Collins has been a director of photography for thirty years. In that time, he's helped a lot of directors and sat behind a lot of cameras. Robert designed the look of the eighties by shooting shows like "Miami Vice" and "Hart to Hart."

Robert starts on a film a minimum of two to three weeks before principal photography starts, but he prefers more time. He says preparation is very important. In the time he has before shooting begins, Robert hires his assistant cameramen and his gaffer, who then hire their own crews. (The gaffer's job is discussed in Chapter 4.)

After the crews are taken care of, Robert talks with the director about the film. Since the director and the DP are the two who really design the color and feel and mood of a film, it is important that they always have a line of communication open. Even if they disagree with each other's ideas, they cannot function independently. Robert talks to his director about the story they are trying to tell. He makes his lighting determination based on that story and instructs his gaffer on what types of lighting instruments to rent for the shoot. The instruments go a long way in creating a distinct lighting pattern or "look" for each film.

Finally, Robert goes out to the locations himself and takes test shots, trying to eliminate as many variables as he can. For a director of photography, variables include film stock, natural light versus artificial, what kind of lens to use, and whether there is room to put the camera on a dolly or if it's got to be handheld. As many of these that can be determined before the entire crew arrives, the faster the shot can be set up and filmed.

Once filming starts, the director of photography adjusts the earlier determinations and makes final decisions on how the camera is going to move and what is going to be included in the shot. Robert says the best thing to learn is, "Show just what you want to see. There is no substitute for actually looking for what to shoot. You want all your pictures to tell the story you are trying to tell." After you can "see" the shot, then you learn how to use the camera to make sure you get it. The more you do it, the more you learn. Robert has three Emmy awards to his credit, and he hasn't stopped learning yet.

## Head Camera Operator

While the director of photography is in charge of what the camera does, the head camera operator is the person who actually sits behind the camera and looks through the lens. It's the operator's job to keep the actors in frame by panning and tilting the camera to follow them. Panning is a side-to-side movement, and tilting is up and down. Both are controlled from the camera mount by either rods or wheels, depending on the type of mount that's being used.

The camera operator makes sure everything looks all right from the camera's point of view. The operator can tell when the shot works and when it doesn't from a strictly visual point of view. On a low-budget film, the DP often doubles as a camera operator to keep the production's costs down. Currently, there is a crop of directors who like to operate their own cameras, Steven Soderbergh being the primary example. He was behind the camera for his Academy Award–winning film *Traffic* as well as the gang heist film *Ocean's 11*.

## First Assistant Camera Operator

The head camera operator handles a lot of the camera movement stuff, but what about focus? If he or she is looking through the viewfinder doesn't the head operator have to keep the actors in focus?

No. That's not the head camera operator's job.

On a film, focus is a critical element. Directors of photography have lost their jobs because the film was out of focus. Because of this, focus on a movie camera has become a precise science, all figured out by distance. The first assistant camera operator, who always carries a measuring tape, will measure the distance from the camera to the actor during the first camera blocking. If the actor moves during the scene, the first assistant camera operator, or first AC, will get measurements at all the key points, then approximate the fill-in numbers to ensure proper focus. It's not easy. A first AC has to have an incredible sense of spatial relations.

In a nutshell, the first AC takes care of the camera. She or he will clean it, load the film magazines onto it, and take notes on each shot and foot of film that passes through it. The camera is the first AC's baby.

## Second Assistant Camera Operator

The second assistant camera operator, otherwise known as the second AC, gets the grunt work of keeping track of how much film stock is left, what kind it is, and in what configurations. Film comes in different speeds for shooting under different conditions, such as day or night. It also comes in two roll sizes. A four-hundred-foot roll will shoot for a little more than four minutes, and a thousand-foot roll gives you just about ten. The second AC needs to know what's left in stock on the camera truck at any given moment and when to order more.

The second AC also gets to do all the official paperwork. This means that all the camera reports, detailing which shots the director liked and wanted printed, and even the camera department's time cards, are all filled out by the second AC. It may not be great, but if you want to be a camera operator, it's where you have to start.

## Clapper and Film Loader

If there's a clapper and film loader on the film, then the second AC is not the entry-level job. Often, though, the duties of the clapper and loader are filled by the second AC. Being a clapper and loader can be fun. After all, you're the only member of the camera crew to, unintentionally, end up on film.

The clapper part of the job means using a clapboard to identify the scene and take numbers for the editor and provide a sound sync noise for the sound editor. The clapboard, which is also referred to as a slate or sticks, is the small slate with the black-and-white sticks on the top. When a scene is slated, the clapper holds the clapboard with the top stick raised, then says the scene number, followed by the take number. If there is more than one camera, the clapper says which camera is being slated (the main camera is always A camera, and the others follow alphabetically). The slate ends with the clapper saying "Mark," and slamming the sticks shut so they make a loud crack.

When editing, the sound of the sticks coming together will match up with the audio tape of the same scene and take. This way, the sound and visuals will be coordinated. If for some reason the scene couldn't be slated at the beginning of the shot, tail sticks are used. Tail sticks are done the same way, with the exception of the clapboard being held upside down and the clapper starting off the verbal slate with the words "tail sticks."

The loader part is just what it sounds like. When all the film comes in from the film company, it's in a can. The loader has to take it into the darkroom and load it into the camera's magazine cartridges. At the same time, he or she has to unload the exposed film and load it into lightproof canisters, ready to be sent to the lab for processing.

## Checking the Gate

Often, while watching a behind-the-scenes featurette about the making of a film, you'll hear someone on set say, "Check the gate." What does that mean?

It means to look into the "gate" that the film passes through on the camera to ensure it's clean. Sometimes a hair or a piece of dust can get in there, which could ruin a series of takes and require the whole thing to be reshot. Checking the gate is the last thing done before the camera is moved to a new location.

## Still Photographer

When you read a review of a film in the newspaper and you see a photograph of a scene from that film, you probably are looking at the still photographer's work—but only a single frame of it. The still photographer is on the film from the first day of shooting and works right alongside the camera crew, capturing select moments of action while the camera crew captures everything.

The still photographer is first and foremost a photographer, with all the background and training that goes along with that. Marie Pfieffer has been taking pictures since she stumbled into a photography elective in high school. Since then, Marie has amassed an impressive portfolio of images, both of her own design and from the various productions she's worked on.

Part of Marie's job requires her to take pictures mimicking what the director of photography sees. She takes pictures of all the scenes as they're being shot, and these are used as part of the publicity packet. Because Marie's camera is always present, her candid snapshots are also used as a double check for continuity. Additionally, she sets up posed publicity stills that enable her to strut her artistic stuff. These are the specialized photos showing characters together who may never appear that way in the film—enemies arm in arm and smiling.

For each of these, Marie needs special equipment, which the production rents from her in the form of a kit or camera rental fee. Some of the equipment Marie uses for her posed shots includes a series of flashes, umbrella reflectors, diffusion screens, and stands—and that doesn't include her cameras. Marie usually has at least two of her eight different camera bodies with her at any time, as well as an assortment of lenses ranging from a 16 mm wide angle to a 1000 mm telephoto, which she uses when she can't get close to her subject. Marie also has an autowinder motor that she can attach to the bottom of her camera for fast action sequences and a device called a blimp that completely covers the camera, deadening any noise that may come from it, which she uses when she's snapping a dialogue scene and her camera noise would be picked up by the sound crew.

The weirdest thing Marie says she's ever had to do was learn how to scuba dive and get underwater housings for her cameras so she could take stills for a short shooting off the California coast. As for getting started, she suggests that you take as many pictures as you can. Build a portfolio showing you can take commercial shots just as easily as artistic ones. Portraiture is also a nice addition, but just take pictures and let people see them. Every film needs a still photographer, so why shouldn't it be you?

# Boom Operator

This person's job is to make sure you can hear the actors. The tool used to do this job is the boom microphone. The boom, invented by Carroll Pratt in the early 1900s, is a rather unique piece of equipment. Basically, it's a microphone on the end of a long pole. The operator holds it above the heads of the actors, out of frame, so the sound mixer can record it. Sound easy? Not really.

First, if the scene is long, the operator must hold the boom for the duration. And holding it is only part of the job. The boom operator needs to know the script fairly well to be able to move the boom from actor to actor as the dialogue happens. If you still think this doesn't sound so bad, take your broom, tie a small weight to the end with the bristles, and hold it by the other end above your head for seven to ten minutes. Now add in the factor of twisting it toward the actors and following them around the scene. That's roughly the idea, if you're lucky. Sometimes, because of the way the scene is set up, the operator may have to use a boom over ten feet long.

The boom operator works closely with the location sound mixer on duties such as microphone selection and placement and gathering ambient sound for background noise. It is partly the boom operator's responsibility to listen as the scene is happening for disturbances such as airplanes or other noises not wanted over the dialogue as well as to make sure there are no shadows getting in the way of the lights. A boom operator can move up the ranks to become a mixer after time and a lot of work.

## Location Sound Mixer

The sound for a film is recorded live on location. Often, parts of it are replaced in postproduction and mixed together to form the final, "sweetened" sound track you hear in the theater. But there's something special about that raw sound, capturing the feeling of the location. The credit for that belongs to location sound mixers.

Location sound is responsible for making sure all dialogue is recorded properly. The mixer needs to know how microphones work and how they need to be placed on an actor to make the best recording. Before the scene starts, the sound mixer and the boom operator (on a big-budget, union film, the mixer supervises the boom operator) wire the actors, if possible, with lavalier microphones. These are small microphones that can be concealed beneath the actor's clothing but still pick up all of the dialogue. The skill comes in knowing how these should be placed so they don't pick up the additional sounds of breathing or the rustle of clothing. While these may seem natural to us, to a sound mixer, they are to be avoided like the plague. The dialogue needs to be recorded crisply so it can be used. Any additional noise (like rustling clothes) can be added later if desired. This way, all the levels can be controlled, and the best sound quality can be achieved.

Sometimes, because of extenuating circumstances beyond anyone's control, a line cannot be recorded cleanly during actual filming. What then? Then you record it separately. This is called a wild line, and the sound mixer asks the actor to say just the line that is needed. Generally, the wild lines are recorded at the same time and in the same place as the regular dialogue. This way, the background, or ambient, noise will be the same.

The sound mixer will even record thirty seconds or more of just ambient noise, which is known as a room tone, for the same reason. In both cases, it provides a constant background for editing. Any room you enter has its own tone. A tile-floored bathroom, for example, will echo louder than a room with wood paneling and wall-to-wall carpeting. Outdoor locations also have a tone, be it the chirping of birds or the almost silent reverberations off a rock wall. The reason for all this ambient noise makes itself known in postproduction. If the dialogue editor clips a section of dialogue, the tape replacing it needs background so there isn't a big empty space, which can be quite distracting.

The location mixer records all of these sounds using either a portable quarter-inch tape recorder, called a Nagra, or, more common these days, a DAT digital recorder. Depending on the type used, it can record up to four separate tracks. So if there are four actors, each one will have her or his own audio track. For a standard location, the recorder is on a sound cart with a place to hold the boom, extra tape, and cables, but the portability of the recorder lets the sound mixer take it over the shoulder to record anywhere.

## Foley Artist

Sound effects are any sounds that are not produced live on location. Sounds that never existed in the real world get created, and things recorded live that don't work get redone in the studio. On big-budget films, most of the sound effects, with the exceptions of guns being fired and large explosions, are recorded on a Foley stage.

A Foley stage is a large, soundproof room designed to recreate real-world sounds, and the Foley artist is the person who uses it. John Roesch is one of the best in Hollywood. He describes his job like this: "Foley is the re-creation of sound effects in sync with the picture used to replace or enhance the production sound."

The first thing you notice walking onto a Foley stage is the floor. The floor is covered by all sorts of different flooring materials, from cobblestone to wooden planking to concrete and even occasionally grass. The floors all simulate other environments. If the scene is a man walking down wooden steps, then John will watch the action on a big-screen monitor and mimic the action he sees. His footsteps will replace the footsteps of the man walking down the steps.

But the floors aren't the only thing around. John renovated the stage at the studio where he works to make it exactly to his liking. So on John's stage not only will you find all the floorings to cover almost any surface you can think of, but also a small pool, which can be filled with water, and rows and rows of hand props.

"The problem with most stages," John says, "is there aren't enough props." And John should know. He's been walking on Foley stages for twenty-five years, and several of his films have won Academy Awards for sound, including *E.T.*, *Raiders of the Lost Ark,* and *The Matrix.* John spent weeks just moving props into his studio. With these hand props, which are used on almost every show he does, and the bigger props in the back storage rooms, used for a number of shows as well, he can recreate anything. There are different kinds of chain in the "chain" bin. The refrigerator (which works but makes too much noise while taping is going on) is used to make refrigerator noises. Any type of metal you can name is represented somewhere, and the difference between two rifles being cocked is apparent right away when you listen to both at the same time. The sound of the jet pack winding down in *The Rocketeer* was created by John on a machine he had built to do nothing but run different motors.

John's ultimate goal is to make the viewer unaware of anything being done to the sound. He wants you to completely believe in the scene you're watching, and he'll go to great lengths to do it. For the Steven Seagal film *Under Siege*, a film where the action takes place on a navy ship, John went out to the Long Beach Naval Yard, where an aircraft carrier was being dismantled, and picked up props so his sounds would be authentic.

Ideally, the way John works is to get a copy of the film to watch all the way through once the picture is locked. This means all the editing is done, and all he has to worry about is getting the sound right.

Then he and his crew—Mary Jo Lang, who is the Foley mixer and records all of what's going on, and Rick Canelli, who is the recordist and is in charge of setting up the tapes and logging which sounds are done and which need to be—start recording. The first thing to be recorded are the footsteps. They go through the entire film recording only the sound of people's feet: running, walking, skipping, shuffling, dancing. Any time feet move, John is there to capture it.

Once feet are finished, the team goes back in and adds all the other things John's studio is set up to do: gates closing, water running, bullets being ejected from a gun—anything that will add reality and believability to the final product. A full-length feature film will take about three weeks to complete, working five days a week, eight hours a day. The good news is that Foley artists can make $500 a day or more.

In certain situations, the actual Foley walker is being replaced by digital Foley effects. For low-budget filmmakers, their fingers walking over a control board and a bank of recorded noises is less expensive than hiring someone like John. But it still doesn't beat the real thing. Just shut your eyes and listen for the difference.

......................

# Composer

At this point, soundwise, the film is almost ready to go. The only element missing is the score. A sound track can consist of a variety of elements, and most people think automatically of the hit song played over the end credits. Yes, that song is part of the film's overall sound track, but then so are the sound effects and the Foley additions we've already talked about.

The most important part of the sound track, however, is the score. This is the background music, which you may not really notice, at least on a conscious level, but which you will definitely miss if it's taken out. The score helps set the mood of the scene as much as the set design or the lighting does. Mostly, it underscores the scene, hence its name, like an underline or italics in a book. The music can punch up the comedy or heighten the dramatic tension. Remember the low, ominous strings from the opening of *Jaws*? How many people can sing the "ee ee ee" from the shower sequence in *Psycho*? That's the score at work.

It can even be used to offset the scene, to give it surreal qualities that the visuals alone can't provide, such as circus music during a grotesque murder sequence. Imagine watching the famous ear-cutting scene from *Reservoir Dogs* without "Stuck in the Middle with You" playing in the background, and you'll see what I mean.

Somebody has to hear all of this in his or her head. The images need to provide the inspiration for a certain series of notes or chords. Patrick Moraz, former keyboard player for rock groups The Moody Blues and Yes, can do it. He has done it for such films as *Predator* and *The Stepfather*.

To start, Patrick talks with the director and reviews the script. "Every element can give seed to ideas," he says. At this point, he starts creating, in very rough forms, the various cues needed for the film. A cue is a section of music used to cover a particular scene or sequence of events, and a film can have anywhere from ten to more than a hundred cues.

With his rough cues in place, Patrick begins to see the dailies of each previous day's work. Using these as his guidelines, he revises his initial cues and creates a complete sonic environment and vocabulary. After watching an actor's performance, Patrick will give him or her a musical signature, a set of notes to correspond to that character. This way, whenever the character appears, the music will incorporate the signature within the cue. The most well-known example of this is the music of *Peter and the Wolf* by Prokofiev. Even certain settings can have their own signatures. In *The Stepfather*, the apartment house has its own notes to identify it.

Electronic music is the direction in which things are going, and the software available to composers is becoming more and more complex. Some of it can effectively duplicate a recording studio. In fact, almost all professional recording studios use some kind of MIDI computer system. Patrick writes all of his music on a keyboard and a home Macintosh computer. This lets him keep track of everything. He may see something while driving around that puts a musical idea into his head. He will compose and store it, having it ready to use when the right project comes along.

Patrick does a tremendous amount of research for any project he's involved with. If the film is a period piece, he tries to be as authentic as possible. He also listens to a wide selection of other music because he never knows what the director will want or where those ideas will come from, and the best strategy is to be prepared.

## Scoring Mixer

Once the composer has created his or her masterpiece, it's up to the scoring mixer to record it. Well, maybe not actually record it, but at least put it on tape and make it sound good. The scoring mixer is the person who organizes the musicians in the recording studio and works with the composer and music producer. Is it any wonder scoring mixer Avi Kipper says that one of the most important aspects of the job is diplomacy?

Even with heavy diplomacy, being a scoring mixer is not an easy gig to get. There are far more jobs for assistants than for mixers themselves, so, obviously, the more you know about everyone else's job, the better. That way you can always be working somewhere in the recording booth.

The nice thing about being a scoring mixer is that you don't need an extensive musical background to do it, just a love of music. An electronic background, however, is very desirable. If you have any experience with ham radios or computers, you're starting off right. Then, when you've decided on mixing as a career, start learning whatever you can about the technology being used in the recording industry. Read all the industry magazines you can get your hands on so you'll be able to at least identify the equipment when you see it. If you can learn how to fix the instruments you'll be using, that skill makes you that much more employable.

But all of that can be done on your own. For advanced learning, check out places like the University of Miami and other larger schools for their recording arts degree programs. With this job, you're flying by the seat of your pants, so it's best to be as well primed as possible.

. . . . . . . . . . . . . . . . . . . . . . . . . . . . . . . . . . . . . . . . . . . . . .

## For Further Information

Images are what people remember most from the films they see—images and sound bites. There are entire books written just with quotes or still pictures from films. There are also a number of books and magazine articles written for those who want to produce those images and sound bites and those who already do.

### Books

Alton, John. *Painting with Light*. New York: Macmillan.

*American Cinematographer Film Manual, 8th Edition*. Los Angeles: The ASC Press.

Bloedow, Jerry. *Filmmaking Foundations.* Burlington, MA: Elsevier Science/Harcourt.

Borwick, John. *Microphone Technology and Technique.* Burlington, MA: Elsevier Science/Harcourt.

Brown, Blain. *Motion Picture and Video Lighting.* Burlington, MA: Elsevier Science/Harcourt.

Carlin, Dan Sr. *Music in Film and Video Production.* Burlington, MA: Elsevier Science/Harcourt.

Cheshire, David. *The Book of Movie Photography.* New York: Alfred A. Knopf, Inc.

*Elements of Color in Professional Motion Pictures.* White Plains, NY: Society of Motion Picture and Television Engineers.

Elkins, David E. *Camera Assistant's Manual.* Burlington, MA: Elsevier Science/Harcourt.

Frayne, John G., and Halley Wolfe. *Elements of Sound Recording.* New York: John Wiley & Sons, Inc.

Hagen, Earle. *Scoring for Films.* Hialeah, FL: Columbia Pictures Publications.

Honore, Paul M. *A Handbook of Sound Recording.* Cranbury, NJ: A. S. Barnes and Company.

Limbacher, James L. *Film Music.* Metuchen, NJ: Scarecrow Press, Inc.

Lyver, Des. *Basics of Video Sound.* Burlington, MA: Elsevier Science/Harcourt.

Malkiewicz, Kris. *Cinematography.* New York: Simon & Schuster.

Mascelli, Joseph V. *Five C's of Cinematography.* Beverly Hills, CA: Silman-James Press.

Mercer, John. *An Introduction to Cinematography.* Champaign, IL: Stipes Publishing Company.

Millerson, Gerald. *Techniques of Lighting for Television and Film.* Burlington, MA: Elsevier Science/Harcourt.

Morgan, David. *Knowing the Score.* New York: Harper Collins.

Sonnenschein, Davis. *Sound Design.* Studio City, CA: Michael Wiese Productions.

Thomas, Tony. *Film Score.* Burbank, CA: Riverwood Press.

Wheeler, Leslie J. *Principles of Cinematography*. New York: Macmillan.

## Magazines

*American Cinematographer Magazine*
1782 North Orange Drive
Hollywood, CA 90028
www.theasc.com/magazine

*Millimeter*
9800 Metcalf Avenue
Overland Park, KS 66212
www.millimeter.com

# CHAPTER FOUR

# Grip and Electric

## A Light Touch

When you're watching a film, most of the departments can be seen or their presence felt just in the pictures—the way the sets look or the way the actors appear. Even the way the images are spliced together has something to say about the final product.

One group of people, however, is critically important, yet you often wouldn't recognize their work. These people are the grips and gaffers. If they weren't around, you'd never have a film finished. These are the unsung heroes of the film industry, the backbone and muscle of any production.

So what is a gaffer? What does a grip do? What is a best boy? This chapter unravels the mystery of these unusual job titles.

## Gaffers

### Lighting Technician

A lighting technician job is the starting point if you eventually want to be a gaffer. However, the title lighting technician is not always used. You may be listed as an electrician or called a juicer. No matter what, you're still doing the same job.

But what is that job? Simply put, you plug things in. The trick, of course, is knowing what to plug in where. This is where experience comes into play. When you get hired on your first film as a lighting technician, you probably won't know much. You may know the difference between an Inky and a One OK (they're both types of lights), but do you know how much power they draw or how far they throw light? Not unless you're coming from a production-oriented film school and maybe not even then.

So how do you learn? You work at it. You ask questions. The gaffer is the one who hires the lighting crew, and most gaffers are willing to answer questions and hire the people who are enthusiastic about the job.

If you don't have a degree in production but you really want to learn the skills of the gaffer, the best way to start is as an intern. Attach yourself to a production for free. Work for the experience, and if you do a good job, the next film just may bring a paycheck and the title lighting technician.

## Best Boy

One of the most fabled jobs in the film industry is the best boy. Many hours of debate have ensued over exactly what it means to be a best boy. Is it that everyone on the set likes you? Are you just great at your job? Can a girl be a best boy? Do you get paid more if you're the best boy? Does it change during the film? If you're having a bad week, does someone else get to be the best boy instead?

The answers: no, no, yes, sometimes, and no. Being a best boy has nothing at all to do with people liking you, or with your age, or with your personality. It's not a contest won weekly by a favored member of the crew. Since it is only a job title, anybody can be a best boy—even a girl. Yes, you get paid more, but only if you started as a lighting technician. Being a best boy is your first promotion. Once you get the job, you keep it for the duration of the project.

After several jobs as a lighting technician, maybe a year or two of working and gaining experience and serving under many different gaffers, you'll get called up out of the ranks to become a best boy. In reality, you become the assistant gaffer. It is up to you to make sure things get done when they are supposed to be done.

During walk-through rehearsals, the best boy becomes a second set of eyes for the gaffer, checking different angles for shadow problems and "kicks," which are hot spots or camera glare causing unwanted glowing. An unnoticed kick can ruin an otherwise perfect take, so it's up to you to help make sure they don't happen.

## Gaffer or Chief Lighting Technician

Well, we're spending a lot of time talking about gaffers. just who are these people who command so much respect from the camera crew? Where do they come from?

Historically speaking, the term *gaffer* comes from live theater and, before that, from fishing boats. It used to be that the running crews of theaters were made up of sailors who were tired of the sea or couldn't get hired on an outgoing vessel. To work on land, they took jobs in local theaters where their talents could be put to use. The reason it's bad luck to whistle in a theater is because the people who ran the rails (ropes that raised and lowered the scenery) got their training by manipulating the riggings on sailing ships. The way they communicated was by whistling. Certain whistles meant certain things, and when they went to work in the theater, they also used whistles, this time to know which piece of scenery to raise or lower. So if you happened to whistle inadvertently, a heavy wooden set piece may have come crashing down on your head. As for gaffers, they did their work with the lights. In the old theaters, the lighting instruments were located high overhead, and the easiest way to focus them or use the "barn doors" (four hinged flaps used to direct the light or cut it off from certain areas) was to reach up with a long stick. Remembering the gaff hooks used when they were fishing, they brought them into the theater and used them to manipulate the instruments. Thus gaffers were born.

Today, they still manipulate lighting, even if they don't use gaff hooks any longer. They're not always called gaffers anymore, either. Sometimes, according to union regulations, the gaffer is called the chief lighting technician. It doesn't matter what you call them, though, the job they do is still the same.

Gene Glick has been doing the job for close to forty years. He started in the old days, during the famed studio system, as a juicer and worked his way up through the ranks until he became a full-fledged gaffer. Everything he learned was filed away, ready to be used again as the situation required.

His job as a gaffer is to make the scene look the way the director and the director of photography want it to look. This means knowing what lights can do and what they can't. A large light (five or ten kilowatt) can adequately light a room (perhaps even overlight it), but so can a group of minis (a smaller instrument). It all depends on the desired effect and what needs to be lit as opposed to what should stay in the shadows. It also depends on what the scene is trying to convey. According to Gene, if the scene is comic, the lights should be bright and cheery. A mysterious scene or a love story will be played more low-key, darker, leaving more to the imagination.

The gaffer's job starts when the set is finished. The gaffer looks at the set and draws up a light plot, a lighting diagram based on the scene to be shot. Gene says one of the biggest problems facing today's gaffers is the abundant use of preexisting, practical sets as opposed to building things specially for a production. "When a set is built by an art director, he knows what types of materials to use to reduce glare, what scenes are going to be played there. He can arrange for walls to be removed easily, rigging to be done from high above where the ceiling would be."

When you have to shoot in an actual room, you don't have the advantage of being able to light from an imaginary vanishing point; you have to make do with what you have. While not building a set may seem cheaper in the beginning, Gene has found it takes him longer to light a practical set, so the savings get eaten up by time.

When the set is lit, the director has a walk-through. While the actors (or their stand-ins) are going through their paces, the gaffer is noting where the shadows are falling and when the actor is or isn't exactly in the light. After a walk-through, Gene always adds more light. You never know quite where things are going to happen, so the initial plan covers the basics, and after the walk-through, things are tweaked to get them just right.

The best thing a gaffer can be is observant. Noticing dark spots and fixing them can make the difference between a good take and a great one. Gene suggests the best thing you can do to be a gaffer is work with as many directors of photography as possible. Get as much experience as you can. And know your lights.

## Rigging Gaffer or Rigger

Remember the light plot from the gaffer section? That's the diagram that shows where all the lighting instruments should be set up to light the scene. The rigging gaffer, or rigger, is the one who reads the plot and makes it happen. If the set is in a studio and the gaffer calls for heavy overhead lights, the rigger either mounts them on preexisting catwalks or builds rigging for them. The same is true of practical sets. The rigger has to figure out how to get all the instruments into whatever space is given to work with.

The rigger has to know how to maximize space and, like the gaffer, has to know the lights. The rigger must be able to let the gaffer know if the instruments asked for can be supported by the structures they need to be mounted on—and if they can't, the rigger must be able to suggest an alternative. In addition to hanging the lights, the rigger attaches gels or places scrims in front of them.

Because the rigger's job could include building things like light trees, trellises, or catwalks or hanging heavy instruments on walls already standing, riggers work closely with the grip department.

**Gels and Scrims.** A gel (short for gelatin, which they used to be made of) is a thin piece of colored plastic that can change the color of the light. If a particular effect is wanted, like giving everything a red tint, a gel is used. Something called a no-color gel is used to bring down the light's temperature. In black-and-white films, gelled instruments were used to create certain visual effects. In monster films, where a transformation on screen was required to make the creature believable, the makeup department would do the actor's normal makeup first, then create the monster look using red-based cosmetics. The lights used to shoot the initial (normal) scene would all have red gels covering them, washing out the monster makeup. When the scene called for it, the gaffer would switch off the red-gelled lights while simultaneously flipping on the scary mood lighting. The ultimate effect was that the red makeup would suddenly become visible, making the actor seem to transform right before the camera lens.

A scrim is a piece of fabric that lets light pass through it from one side and is used to cause a varying amount of diffusion to prevent glare. Depending on the requirements of the scene, diffusion can be used in increments from one-half to two as well as being placed only over selected areas of the instrument. The result is a softer, more pleasant light. Flags look similar to scrims except they are opaque. They are used in much the same way as a barn door on the instrument or like your hand when you try to shade the lens of your camera at home.

## Grips

### Key Grip

If you have an item on set and you need to hide it, move it, or shade it, who are you going to call? The grips. Whatever you need, the grips are there for you. These people are the muscle of the film set. If something needs to be moved and you need a hand, ask a grip. Grips are often working hand in hand with the riggers, setting up stands, putting up flags, and helping out with the lights and camera.

Grips have to know all the equipment on the set and what it's used for. Almost any major city in the country will have a rental house to supply gear and equipment to visiting film crews. Look in your local phone book, find one, and pay a visit. Find out how to use things like C (century) stands, apple boxes, reflectors, and sandbags. Then look into the lights. You may not be responsible for making them work, but as a grip, you'll have to move them, and you'll be really embarrassed if they want a ten kilowatt and you bring over a mini.

The key grip is the head grip, the one who does most of the hiring for the department (the rest is done by the best boy grip, who is the key's assistant) and delegates tasks to the crew on the set. The key grip also handles the renting of equipment. Often, a key who has been in the industry for a while will have accumulated a lot of personally owned equipment and will rent it out to the production company. The advantage of this, besides the key making more money, is knowing the gear. Generally, it will take a number of years before a grip becomes a key. In that time, if the grip has collected all this equipment, he or she knows what is needed and what isn't and won't waste the production's money on unnecessary stuff. The reason the grip will know what is needed is that the grip reads the script and breaks it down for locations and times of day. For shooting outside at night, the key grip knows lights will be needed, and on-the-job experience will give the grip a rough idea of which lights will work best.

In the case of grip work, experience is invaluable, and the only way to get it is to volunteer for a production and work hard.

## Dolly Grip

Once you've mastered the basic grip equipment and you're working on a film, odds are you'll be called in to help lay dolly track. A dolly is a manual camera vehicle, usually a cart with four wheels, used to move the camera forward and backward smoothly. Some dollies have cranes attached for raising or lowering the camera while moving it forward and back. Dolly track is used to limit the dolly's movement to a straight line. It looks like miniature train tracks, and it all has to be level and aligned or the dolly won't be able to go over it.

The dolly grip is the one who actually pushes or pulls the dolly and raises or lowers the crane arm in accordance with what's needed for the shot. A good dolly grip is smooth and powerful, able to drive the dolly to hit the marks and stop it without jarring the camera. For complicated shots, the dolly grip may have to raise the arm while pushing forward along the track, stop, then pull back and lower the arm—all this in one take while the camera's rolling. It takes a lot of practice, but starting as a general grip will put you on the set with the equipment, and all you have to do is ask how to use it.

## Steadicam Operator

The Steadicam is a piece of equipment usually owned by the Steadicam operator, who is hired on a daily basis to come in and film particular scenes. The purpose of a Steadicam is to take the jarring bounce out of handheld shots. It was first used for the famous running-up-the-steps sequence in the original *Rocky* and since then has gone through a couple of different versions and a multitude of uses.

A Steadicam was used for the speeder chase sequence of *Return of the Jedi*. The Steadicam operator walked slowly along a specified path with the camera shooting at extremely slow speed. When processed and shown at the standard twenty-four frames per second, the effect was of something moving very quickly and steadily through the forest.

The Steadicam unit itself is actually a harness with a series of movement-dampening springs and a camera mount. Since each Steadicam is custom fitted for comfort and size, it is very rare that a production can rent just the unit and put it on its own camera operator. Usually, the Steadicam and the operator come as a package, which is beneficial for the production because the operator knows how to use the equipment to get the best shot possible. The operator also knows the limitations and will not do something that could endanger self or gear.

Steadicam makes units for every budget and camera size, whether you need something to keep the a digital video camera steady for a low-budget short or to manage a big, 35 mm movie camera.

....................................................

## For Further Information

The backbone of any production, the grips and gaffers can always use an extra pair of hands. If you don't mind the long hours or the hard work, contact a production and volunteer your services. Everybody has to start someplace, and these people will teach you what they know, as long as you're there, pulling with them.

The following corporations provide information about the products used by gaffers and grips, profiles of professionals in the field, and workshops.

Mole-Richardson Co. Catalog
937 North Sycamore Avenue
Hollywood, CA 90038
www.mole.com

Steadicam
The Tiffen Company, LLC
90 Oser Avenue
Hauppauge, NY 11788
www.steadicam.com

## Books

Taub, Eric. *Gaffers, Grips, and Best Boys*. New York: St. Martin's Press.

Uva, Michael, and Sabrina Uva. *The Grip Book*. Burlington, MA: Elsevier Science/Harcourt.

# CHAPTER FIVE

# Art
## Setting the Scene

W hat is art? Is it the sculpture outside the local bank? How about the painting composed of nothing but different hues of red splotched all over a pink canvas and called *Man in the Time of the Mammoth*, hanging in a local gallery and astronomically priced? Maybe art is the photograph taken by your Aunt Rose of you when you were three.

All these things are art in some form or another. But if you want to belong to the art department of a film crew, you have to know that art is all this and more.

On a film, the art department is responsible for the look of the film. No matter where or when the film is set, the members of the art department work together to create the appropriate environment and atmosphere. This could include anything from building a complete town for a Western to creating a spaceport for a science fiction epic.

In addition to designing and building sets, the art department has the responsibility for what goes on the sets, making sure the table and chairs not only match each other but match the decor of the setting they are in. Members of the art department have to be highly creative to replicate artifacts from the past or future. They also must be historical experts, so they can faithfully recreate any period in history as well as any social class in that period.

The art department is a talented, educated unit. As a group, it has done everything from creating the prehistoric landscape of

*The Flintstones* to the Elizabethan stages of *Shakespeare in Love* to the hi-tech futuristic world of *The Matrix.*

## Art Department Assistant

This is basically the same as a regular production assistant (as described in Chapter 2), but the art department assistant is assigned exclusively to the art department. The art department assistant will learn all aspects of the art department and should be ready and willing to help out wherever needed.

This is a great entry-level position if your talents and desires point in this direction. Once you graduate from being a general assistant, you may become a specialized assistant, as in the case of an assistant prop master, or, if you're lucky and talented, become a full-fledged member of an art department on a feature film.

## Property Custodian/Master

Anything an actor handles in front of the camera is considered a property, or prop. If the actor walks into a room carrying a bottle of soda and sets it down on a table, that bottle falls under the jurisdiction of the property custodian, or prop master. That's it. Now, if you think of some recent films you've seen and what the actors in those films handled, you'll realize being a property custodian is not as easy as it sounds.

David McGuire can tell you for sure. He's been doing property work for more than twenty years. His job starts in preproduction. First, he goes through the script, looking for props. Once he has the actual list, he takes a look at what kind of film it is. For example, if he's doing a biker film, he'll make a list of things not necessarily mentioned but that might be found with these movie bikers. If the film is about bikers in the present, then David can move from here to actually getting the props. But if it's a futuristic biker gang, and the script calls for the lead biker to carry a "Napoleon

Crisis" as a weapon, then David must sit down with the production designer and the film's director to decide what this weapon should look like. Before the meeting, David will know where and how this prop is supposed to play in the scene, and he'll be able to do thumbnail sketches of a couple of ideas to show the people in charge.

Then it's off to buy or fabricate the needed props. In most major cities, there are prop houses. In Los Angeles, there are more than a dozen. These are places where they have stockpiles of props, ranging from plastic fruit to vintage telephones to menu covers and interiors for any style of restaurant with any name you choose. If you don't want to move to Los Angeles but you want to get a prop background, prop houses are a good place to work; check the local Yellow Pages. The great thing about prop houses is they are like supermarkets for prop people, and for a price, they'll even build things they don't normally stock. So David comes here to rent most of his usual props, but since the director isn't quite sure how he wants the Napoleon Crisis to look, David builds three different versions, complete with hollow barrels for the effects crew to rig a laser in. The director likes the second one, so David builds two more, just to be on the safe side. But he doesn't get rid of the other two prototypes; they just go into his kit.

A property custodian's kit, or box, for which he or she gets an extra weekly kit rental fee, is filled with things the prop master has collected over the years: custom-built specialized props, specially designed books and certificates, things that could be used on almost any shoot with just a slight redressing. This is what the rental fee is for: to save time and money by already having it around.

Once the cameras start to roll, things can happen very quickly. The director may ask for some prop to try out an idea for a scene or a suddenly devised bit of action. According to David, "You never say no, but there is always a time-and-money factor. Everything can be done; it's just a matter of how long until you need it and how much money you can spend." The property custodian has to be prepared for all this and more. He or she should have a general knowledge of everything from firearms to table manners. If there is a scene set in a posh restaurant and the table is set with fancy folded napkins, not only should the prop master be able to tell the actor which fork to use and how to use it but also be able to refold the napkin properly when the scene needs to be reshot from a different angle or for a second take.

Finally, the property custodian needs also to be aware of continuity. Since film is shot entirely out of order, a woman walking down the street carrying flowers on the first day of shooting may enter a doorway for which the interior is shot on the last day of shooting, but since it all flows together on the screen, the flowers have to look the same. The property custodian must be aware of what kind of flowers they were, how they were being held, and other such details. This is called continuity, and while there is a person specifically hired to do this job, everyone is responsible for his or her own department. Invest in an instant camera so you always have a reference photo from which to work.

## Dead Alien Babies

The "dead alien baby" principle was learned firsthand by assistant prop master Mark Phillips. The principle goes something like this, according to Mark: "You're doing a Western, and you've got everything the script calls for in the prop truck—everything you could possibly find in a Western even if it wasn't called for in the script. You've got saddles, blankets, rifles, breakaway bottles, those swinging saloon doors—everything. Then, when you get out to the location, fifty miles away from nowhere, the shot is all set up and ready to go, you've got all the props required for the scene out and in place, and just before the camera rolls, the director yells for you to fly in the dead alien baby."

The lesson taught to property custodians by this fable: always be prepared.

# Assistant Property Custodian

The assistant property custodian, or assistant prop master, spends a lot of time on set. Mark Phillips started out as an art department assistant and was promoted to assistant property manager while working on a low-budget film. His job went from general to specific, and he became responsible for having the props on set when the director called for them. He would give them to the actors before the scene started and take them away when the shot was over. Whenever he had spare time, Mark also had to make sure the prop truck was organized so everything was easily found and the props required for the rest of the day's scheduled scenes were readily accessible.

Before the shoot starts, the assistant prop master, if hired for preproduction, will help the prop master acquire and store the props needed. The assistant may even function as a runner, going to the various prop houses to pick things up. If so, the assistant also gets to decide certain things, as Mark did on his last job. Mark's latest film was a rock-and-roll fantasy, and the prop master left the particular brands of instruments up to Mark, especially the guitars, since Mark is himself a guitar player and knows who uses the different types of guitars and why. It worked out well; the director liked Mark's choices. And on his next film, Mark is going to have his first shot at being a prop master.

But Mark also works on low-budget, nonunion films. A union film works a little differently. You still work your way up through the ranks, it just takes a little longer, and you end up being more skilled. You are also better paid. There's something to be said for going either way. At least you're making movies.

# Set Dresser

Let's go back a minute. We said a prop was everything the actor touched. But what about the stuff in the background, the stuff hanging on the walls or sitting on the kitchen counter? Where did that stuff come from, and who is responsible for putting it there? You guessed it: the set dresser. The dresser is who gets to "dress" the set, making the child's room look lived in or the doctor's waiting room look real (leaving the out-of-date magazines lying about).

Sounds easy, doesn't it? Just throw some clothes around, tack up a poster of David Cassidy, and poof!—a teenage girl's bedroom from the early 1970s.

If it were that easy, Jennifer D'Angelo wouldn't find her job as challenging as she does. "I've really got to know my history," she says. For instance, in the bedroom scene of our example, the David Cassidy poster helps define the time, but Jennifer couldn't leave the sound track album from the film *Saturday Night Fever* lying against the record player because the film had not yet been released in the time period this shot took place. Her knowledge is not limited only to things. Decorations are also defined by social status. Take the same teenage girl, same early 1970s time period, but this time show a neat, orderly room with a coming-out dress draped carefully across the four-poster bed; on the walls, framed reproductions of classical paintings; sitting on the bookshelf, a dog-eared copy of *Love Story*. This is the room of a far more affluent individual than the David Cassidy fan.

On a large-scale production, when there is more than one set being constructed at a time, all of them will need to be dressed before they can be shot. Actually, on almost any film, there will be at least one set waiting in the wings while shooting is going on elsewhere. This way, the director doesn't have to waste time waiting for the set to get ready. Each of these sets needs to be dressed. The person coordinating all of the set dressing is the head set dresser, traditionally called the lead man (though it can be a woman). The head set dresser, as supervisor of the group, works directly under the set decorator.

# Set Decorator

The examples discussed in the previous sections work if the room is already built. The job of the set decorator is to guide the work of the dressers as well as to define the physical space of the room to be dressed.

If the film is shooting in a studio, then once the construction crew finishes the walls, the set decorator organizes and oversees the addition of details such as fireplace fronts and shelving units. In short, everything but the walls belongs to the set decorator.

This is true even if the film is using an actual location, such as a house or an office building. The decorator decides if the walls need to be painted a different color or if the fireplace needs to be covered over as if it weren't there.

In each room, the set decorator has worked with the prop master and especially the art director to achieve the correct feel the film's director is going for. Like all aspects of making a film, working on set in the art department requires working as a team.

# Production Designer

Now you've got your team defined. You know who's going to be doing what on set once the production gets rolling. There's only one thing missing: somebody has to pull the entire crew together. That person is the production designer.

When the script comes in, the production designer breaks it down into individual locations. Once this list is complete, or even before, the production designer meets with the director of the film to determine the look, or visual style, that will dominate the film. Odds are, the director will have some definite ideas, and it is the production designer's job to bring them to three-dimensional reality. If the film is about a successful New Jersey mafioso family and the film opens in the home of the head of this family, it is up to the production designer to decide what this home should look like. The director may have already decreed something in a "suburban tacky" style, so the production designer will envision a set to fit the director's vision. To this end, a production designer may also work with a location scout to find existing structures that fit the design without too much adaptation.

If the film is a futuristic fantasy, where nothing that already exists can be used, then everything must be designed from scratch. Entire cities have been built on soundstages in Hollywood, along with alien planets and spaceships. All these things were created using the production designer's designs and blueprints.

A production designer must be able to render ideas into usable forms, like blueprints, and should also have an understanding of construction principles and theory, especially set construction, which differs considerably from actual, practical building.

## Art Director

On a really big film, a production designer will become more of an administrator, delegating many of the practical design aspects of the job to the art director. An art director's job is more directly related to the actual construction of the sets. It falls to the art director to make allowances for minor details, such as tweaking to make sure the molding is right. And if the film's director asks for new construction just before the scene is to be shot, the art director should be ready to perform miracles.

It's not a far step from art director to production designer, and on low-budget films, the two jobs are often combined. A solid background in art and construction techniques is needed for both, plus a vision for how the whole design will appear on film.

## Graphic Artist/Designer

Imagine: You're watching a film, and the main character wants to go to an island paradise that doesn't really exist but plays an integral part in the story. She does her research on the Internet, finding out all about this place. Then she walks into a travel agency and sees a poster on the wall, advertising this fantasy land. She books her trip.

Now the question is: who created this island? The graphic designer did. On smaller-budget films, this job falls to the prop master, but on big-budget shoots, this could be one person or an entire crew.

The graphic designer could also be responsible for creating logos, computer displays, and flyers the lead character hands out. Graphic designers work closely with the production designer and the director to make sure everything has the same feel. An art and graphics background is helpful to gain the skills needed to give the director plenty of design options. And when it comes to making up an island getaway, just think of the research involved.

. . . . . . . . . . . . . . . . . . . . . . . . . . . . . .

## Storyboard Artist

Storyboards have been used for years by top-name directors and are now becoming a standard within the industry. Walt Disney and Alfred Hitchcock both used them. Most of the top directors working today, such as Katherine Bigelow and Steven Spielberg, use them. But what are they?

Storyboards are a series of panel (or frame) drawings that accurately depict the action of the film. It's like a comic book for the director to follow. In fact, the artist has to know as much about the process of filmmaking as the director does to be good at the job. Most directors would rather work with someone who has a little artistic talent and a lot of filmmaking ability than the other way around. The art can always be learned and refined, but knowing the camera angles and continuity is the hard part.

You must have a passion for film, because as a storyboard artist, you are an integral part of the production. You take the script, read it, and after talking it over with the director, basically film it with your pencil. You can be on the film from before it starts (your panels can be used to budget the film) until principal photography ends. This can involve as much as eight months and take you to places as far away as Italy or Japan.

The panels themselves vary in size but are usually four by six inches. The artist can describe the entire action of the movie with these, including camera movements and optical tricks like dissolves and wipes. There are literally thousands of panels drawn for a single feature, with new panels being added on a weekly basis. Every time something changes in the film, the storyboard artist must create new boards to cover it. The artist is expected to draw between thirty and thirty-five panels a day, depending on the style of art the director requires.

Since most storyboards are done in black and white, the artist should be well versed in pencil techniques as well as pen-and-ink and marker. The best storyboard artists may be paid up to $2,000 a week in town and more if they are asked to leave home for any period of time. But don't expect to jump right in to these highly coveted assignments. It all takes work and perseverance and more work. Your best bet to begin is by contacting commercial or video production facilities, as well as film houses, since all three use storyboard artists. Any credit is a good credit, and credits are what people look for.

To get started, reading *Film Directing Shot by Shot* by Steven D. Katz and drawing a few storyboards are good openers. If you can get hold of a screenplay, that's great, but if you can't, pick up any action-adventure novel and board an action sequence from it. If it takes half a day to do fifteen panels, you're in the running.

## Production Illustrator

A production illustrator works very closely with the art director or production designer. The illustrator takes the concepts and blueprints from the set designers and realizes them in full-color renderings. This work can be used in several ways.

If the production is already in full swing, then the production illustrator's work is used as a guide for the painters and construction crew so they can see the finished product. If the production is still trying to get off the ground, a producer will bring in a production illustrator to create elaborate scenes from the proposed film in the hopes of attracting investors. Either way, the illustrator creates gorgeous, presentation-quality pieces of artwork in full color.

## Construction Crew

Before an actor can take a long walk through the corridors of a spaceship on its way to Alpha Centauri and a rendezvous with some alien creature intent on destroying Earth, that spaceship needs to be built. We've already talked about how it gets to look like a spaceship on the inside, but all those people need a structure on which to hang the instrument clusters and buttons and lights to make the ship look precisely the way the production designer designed it.

### Carpenter

The carpenters, or hammers, as they're called by those in the know, are the ones who do all the hard work. Officially—that is, according to the union—carpenters are classified as prop makers with a specialization for movies. Even though they are not prop masters, carpenters are given this designation because when the union was first organizing, there was a problem with actual carpenters wanting the film jobs, and what film carpenters do is quite a bit different from regular carpentry. Ask Frank Leasure; that's how he started out in the film industry. His early construction gigs included building huts and booths for the Southern California Renaissance Pleasure Faire, and his work there led him directly to film. Once he was making films, Frank's experience in re-creating the period look of the Renaissance helped out immensely, because for construction in the movies, the most important thing is to make it look right. According to Frank, all of what you see on the screen is fakery, and 70 percent of that is jury-rigged just long enough to get the shot. After the scene is in the can, the set comes down and the next one is built.

The carpenters also work with the prop master when it comes to building props, which is where the union designation comes from. They build the props that are large pieces and require significant construction.

But don't get your hopes up about hanging out with the big celebrities. When you work construction, you may start building a set as much as five months (or more) before that set is scheduled to work (be shot).

If you're lucky, you'll have a friend, as Frank did, to pull you into the industry. If not, your best bet is to learn as much about woodworking and cabinetry as you can. Cabinetry is useful because a lot of what you'll be doing is finishing work, making things look as if they were real and usable.

You can build up your contacts by taking jobs in commercial houses. These are places that produce television commercials. If you live in Los Angeles, New York, Vancouver, Toronto, or any of the other major production centers, there will be several commercial houses around, but even if you don't live in a major entertainment center, there has to be somebody (probably several somebodies) producing local commercials. Build your resume with them.

## Swing Gang Member

If you want to hang out with famous celebrities, then you want to be a member of the swing gang. These people are still part of the construction crew, and they still have to do all the same type of work the hammers do. The main difference is that they get to do it on set while the show is filming. This means they have to work closely with the director, who may ask for things not on the original blueprints. One story related by Frank, who moved from carpenter to swing gang, told how the carpenters had put in a nonfunctioning door frame on a wall in a barn set to kind of spruce things up. The director liked it so much, he wanted the gang to make it a functional doorway. They did, only now, when the door was opened, you could see the wall of the soundstage. The gang put in a false wall to back up the door so it looked real. Problem solved—until the director wanted to walk the camera down the hallway and through the door, which officially wasn't supposed to be there. When it was all done, the gang had built a complete hallway, including hanging walls over ten feet in the air (the doorway was on the second floor), as well as the door.

## Gang Boss

The gang boss is the sergeant of the construction crew. Also known as the pusher, the gang boss organizes the crews. On a big-budget film, where there may be more than one stage working at any given moment, there will be a gang boss on each stage, covering each set. This is their world, and they are in charge when it comes to the construction teams. The gang boss is there to answer questions and make snap decisions.

In the case of the extra doorway, the gang boss had to make the decisions on materials and colors for walls that no one had designed. If there's time, the boss will consult with superiors—the art director or the construction coordinator—but mostly, the prompt decisions are made solo.

## Construction Coordinator

Frank's next promotion was to construction coordinator. The nearest nonindustry equivalent for the coordinator is the job of general contractor. The construction coordinator works right under the art director and is responsible for going through the blueprints, deciding how much wood or paint is going to be needed, and ordering it. The coordinator also has the task of assembling the crews for each particular set and overseeing their work to ensure that it is completed on time. In other words, the coordinator is more of a set manager, a liaison between the crews and the design team.

## Greens Planter

As far as specialized jobs go, greens planter ranks right up there as one of the most specialized. The job of a greens planter, as you might imagine, involves plants.

The greens planter makes sure the grass is green, the trees have leaves, and the plants are all in bloom, if that is what the script calls for. If the script calls for a dead oak with branches arranged in the shape of letters to warn off the hero, then the greens planter must provide that. No matter the season or weather, the plants have to look right. If you're shooting a scene in Southern California that actually is supposed to take place on the East Coast, then the greens planter must make sure there are no palm trees, or anything else that doesn't belong, in the shot. If there are palm trees in the way, the greens planter must dress them so they look like trees that are found naturally in the area where the film is supposed to take place.

Greens planters have been known to do things like staple leaves to trees in the winter to simulate summer as well as spray paint green leaves orange and brown and red to simulate a New England fall in the heat of a Los Angeles summer. There have even been times when a greens planter had to lay grass rugs to make the yard look well cared for.

All of the major Hollywood studios have their own greenery departments and plant nurseries. It is not uncommon, when wandering around a back lot, to see a huge elm tree on rollers being taken off to a set somewhere to fill out a scene. In addition to the studio route, there are many nurseries, especially near major production centers, that rent plants and trees for a production.

Most greens planters come from a nursery background and know plant life. It is the type of job that is passed on from parent to child, but if you want to pursue it, a degree in botany would be a good start.

......................

# Painting Crew

## Painter

Painting can be complex or extremely simple, depending on the task you're assigned to do. Almost anybody can pick up a roller or a brush and make a wall a different color, and this is what a lot of painting is about. When the construction crew is finished, the painters come in and make everything the color it's supposed to be. But what happens when there is supposed to be a marble pillar supporting a vase in the background, and the construction crew built a wooden pillar instead? Then the painter has to marbleize it. Marbling is a talent painters must know.

There are other tricks as well. Wood-grain painting or dry brush techniques are both common illusions painters are called on regularly to create. It is best to familiarize yourself with the multitude of things that can be done with your brush before you sign on as a painter.

## Paint Foreman

Like the construction coordinator, the paint foreman is the man (or woman, despite the sexist title) who coordinates the painters. He or she assigns the tasks and works with the construction coordinator on the ordering of paints and materials.

## Scenic Artist

A scenic artist has the biggest job in the paint department: doing the backdrops—the big backdrops, the ones that take up an entire wall. These are the backdrops used to simulate landscapes, skylines, or cityscapes. A scenic artist takes a small idea for a backdrop and enlarges it.

The scenic artist works with something known as a paint frame, which is a large frame on hydraulics on which the canvas is hung. The thing that separates this from an ordinary easel, besides size, is the way it works. The scenic artist can stand at ground level and have the paint frame raise or lower the canvas up to thirty feet either way. The artist can then work on any section without worrying about ladders or rehanging the painting. If Michelangelo had had something like this, he never would have gotten paint in his eyes.

In Los Angeles, there are specific companies that do nothing but backdrops and scenic paintings, and almost all production companies go through them rather than hire a scenic artist for any specific production.

## Sign Writer/Painter

Picture this: The main character is walking around a back lot set up to look like a downtown area. In her hand is a crumpled-up piece of paper with the name of a business. She sees it, written in fancy letters, arched in a semicircle in the front window of the shop. She goes inside, and the scene continues. But if that shop doesn't already exist, someone has to design and letter the shop window. That's the job of the sign writer, or sign painter.

While the pay is better than that for the average painter, the job difficulty is also greater. A sign writer should know how to letter in a number of fonts (type styles) as well as how to create effects such as drop shadows or italics or, like in the example, writing in a semicircle. The sign painter is responsible for all the signs in the film, whether they are signs painted on glass on the front window of a shop, street signs, or even placards announcing the end of the world. A good design sense is a definite asset, as is a sense of the typefaces of history—you're not going to want a futuristic font on a Western's wanted poster.

The sign writer works with the prop crew on some of this but is generally considered part of the paint crew. This means a sign painter also needs to know all the things a painter should know as well as the specialized lettering techniques unique to the trade. The paint crew is the way to start for this job, and if you're good, the possibilities for advancement will never stop.

## For Further Information

You've decided that the Hollywood art world is for you, but where do you find more information on your chosen field? Try these books. They'll all provide deeper insight into what you're getting yourself into.

Begleiter, Marcie. *From Word to Image*. Studio City, CA: Michael Wiese Productions.

James, Thurston. *The Theater Props Handbook*. Crozet, VA: Betterway Publications.

Katz, Steven D. *Film Directing Shot by Shot*. Burlington, MA: Elsevier Science/Harcourt.

Millerson, Gerald. *TV Scenic Design*. Burlington, MA: Elsevier Science/Harcourt.

Simon, Mark. *Storyboards—Motion in Art*. Burlington, MA: Elsevier Science/Harcourt.

Thomas, James. *Script Analysis for Actors, Directors, and Designers*. Burlington, MA: Elsevier Science/Harcourt.

# CHAPTER SIX

# Makeup and Costumes

## Looking the Part

I s there anyone who hasn't played dress up with a friend at some point in their lives? Put on fancy clothes, extravagant makeup, and done each other's hair to match the shoes? The people in this chapter do it for a living.

Whenever you see someone in a film, what that person is wearing has been, at the very least, approved by the director. At the most, it has been designed and built specifically for the actor who is wearing it. If the movie is a period piece—that is, set in a time period other than the present—all costumes have to be organized to enhance and not destroy the illusion. In a fantastic science fiction film like *Star Wars Episode II: Attack of the Clones* or a historical romance like *Shakespeare in Love*, all the costumes, including those worn by the extras, have to be constructed from scratch.

Now that all of the costumes are taken care of, we need to finish outfitting our heroes. They need to have appropriate hairstyles for a period piece, or perhaps something new and exciting must be created. In *Star Wars*, the outfits and hairstyles worn by Amidala defined her character almost as much as any dialogue she spoke.

It is precisely because of this type of character identification that the director, and often the actor, works very closely with the costume and makeup designers and fabricators. They all work together to bring the total character to life. If anyone falters, the character is the one who suffers.

## Costume Designer

About two-and-a-half months before the film begins shooting principal photography, the costume designer is brought in to dress the characters. Well, not actually dress them, but decide what they are going to be wearing throughout the film. But according to Susan Nininger, who has designed costumes for stars such as Kevin Costner, Robert De Niro, and Whitney Houston, a costume designer does more than that. It is not just one job; it has a lot of components. She describes her career as being part designer, part artist, part psychologist, and part mother.

When Susan gets the script, she reads it through, looking for elements important to her department. Key things she'll notice are the duration of the film (in film time), how many characters need to be outfitted, and any special costuming notes. If the film consists solely of two people talking during a single night in modern times, then there are only two costumes to worry about, and both of them are contemporary, probably things that can be bought off the rack. On the other hand, if the film is a period piece that follows the struggle of a young slave through fifty years of his life, surrounded by a cast of thousands, the costumes will be much more complicated.

Once the script is broken down by character and costume, Susan starts getting ideas. If the film is a period piece, there are several costume research libraries in Hollywood that can give her help in narrowing down periods to specific dates and regions. She jots down notes or creates tear sheets (copies of pictures from books or magazines that show the general idea of what she has in mind) to organize her thoughts, but she won't start designing until she has met with the director.

After meeting with the director (and probably the production designer) and discussing the original costume ideas and how they work with the director's vision, Susan begins sketching. At this point in her design schedule, Susan also tries to talk with the actors she's designing for. She says that building a rapport, a trust, with the actors makes her job much easier. It also allows the actors to contribute some of their own ideas about the costumes and characters.

When her designs are approved, Susan sends them out to be built or goes shopping herself. If the film is contemporary, Susan gets to shop for some of the pieces, then just has them tailored for the actors. On period productions, whatever can't be rented has to be constructed. If she's working on a major studio film, then the studio will have its own costume shop to translate Susan's drawings into apparel. The alternative to the studio shop, if needed, is to take the designs to an independent costumer with his or her own resources. Either way, the costumes are constructed, and the fittings take place.

At the fittings, Susan meets with the actors face-to-face, possibly for the first time. The costumes are donned, and Polaroids are taken. The pictures are a reference for the director. Susan takes notes on how the costumes fit—where things should be tightened or loosened and how the actors feel about them. After the fittings, the changes are made, and the costumes are hung until needed.

When the costumes are needed, Susan is there on the set. She makes sure she is there on the first day any particular costume works (is worn on film). She needs to be on hand in case something goes wrong. It doesn't happen often, but things change from moment to moment, and an outfit that may have worked beautifully in daylight may not look right under the shooting conditions. Susan will be able to fix any of these problems and get the costumes established. Once established—once they've been filmed—and any other time you see them, they have to be the same to ensure continuity.

Being a costume designer is not something you can start out doing. Susan has a fine arts background and has worked hard to get where she is today. Along the way, she's done all the jobs that lead up to hers and learned a lot of skills. The basics include dyeing, cutting, and sewing all sorts of fabrics. You can learn these skills at a design school, and that will help you get started, but it's all those parts (designer, artist, psychologist, and mother) that will keep you going in the career.

## Costume Supervisor

The costume supervisor works for the designer and acts as a liaison between the designer and the key costumers. On the set, the supervisor oversees all the costumes, handling any problems that might arise. If there are any changes that need to be made and the designer is not available, the supervisor is there to accomplish them.

The most important function of the costume supervisor, though, is to handle the paperwork. The supervisor is responsible for any costume reports generated by the department, as well as being the funnel of information from the set to the designer and vice versa.

## Key Costumer

If you can sew and want to meet celebrities, this may be the place for you. Key costumers are the backbone of the costume department. They are responsible for the day-to-day work on the set. The costume designer may be there the day the costume is established, but the keys have to maintain the piece once it has been seen. If the film is shooting for several weeks, and the actors are wearing the same things in every shot, this kind of maintenance can be extremely important.

The reason the keys repair and service the costumes as needed is that another part of the job is continuity. Costumes have to look the same from shot to shot, even if they're damaged. If they don't look the same, the audience will spend time watching for costume mistakes rather than enjoying the film.

But the real fun of being a key costumer is that you get to work with the stars on a daily basis. You make sure that the stars' costumes for the day are neatly pressed and hanging in their trailers when they arrive. You tell them which costume to put on for the next scene and teach them how to wear their period outfits. You may get to help them dress. Whenever an actor calls for someone to zip them up, there you are.

The keys are not designers, but they need to know how things are put together so they can repair anything that breaks. Buttons that fly off need to be reattached, and pant legs constantly need to be hemmed. And wherever these things are being done, you can usually find a costumer, holding a needle loosely in his or her lips, ready to take care of it.

···························

## Makeup Artist

When the actors report for the day, one of the first places they hit, after the craft service table, is the makeup department. Everybody on camera has to wear some makeup, even if it's just to bring out the person's natural color under all the lights.

If the scene calls for a high-society party or a prehistoric tribal gathering, then the makeup on the leads should reflect that. It is up to the makeup artist to apply the actors' makeup in the morning and touch it up as the day goes on.

William "Billy" Thomasson didn't want to get involved with makeup, but when he did, he hit the ground running. "Originally, I wanted to be an actor. I was going to college as a drama major and had to take a makeup class as part of my course requirement. I didn't want to learn anything about makeup; I thought it was something for girls to put on me while I was in my star trailer.

"The first day of class, in staggers the professor, looking all beat-up," Billy recalls. "He had a black eye, and his nose was bleeding and looked broken. When he collapsed in front of the podium, we all rushed to help him. Somebody asked him what had happened, and he said he had a real nasty run-in with a makeup brush. Then he got up, grabbed a jar of cold cream and cleaned himself up. I knew then this was going to be an interesting class."

Billy went from one class in makeup to a complete course in cosmetics. He started out working for photographers on print ads and then came to Los Angeles to do films.

As a makeup artist for feature films, Billy works with the director and the production designer to create a makeup look for the film. He'll also work with the costume designer to make sure the colors and designs he wants to use will go with the costumes.

Billy can create any era of time and any class level needed for the project, from the down-and-out unemployed in the 1930s to the aristocratic French in the 1700s. If he doesn't know the appropriate makeup style offhand, he researches it to make sure he gets it right. He specializes in flat, everyday makeup but has been known to design his share of black eyes and bloody noses.

## Hairdresser

What do you do when you hire a long-haired guy to play a 1920s private detective? Knowing that men in the 1920s, especially private detectives, didn't have long hair, you send him to see the hairdresser, who will cut and style his hair so he looks as if he just stepped out of a 1922 advertisement for hair cream. If the filming takes several months, he will need to make repeated trips to the hairdresser.

But that's not all. Sure, a hairdresser needs to be certified as a hairdresser, which means passing the state's exams and more than likely a few years in beauty school, but that only covers actual hair. On a film, the hairdresser is also responsible for any wigs an actor wears. Being responsible means not only purchasing them or having them built but also maintaining and styling them as needed. Anything special done to the hair, such as braids or ponytails, is the hairdresser's responsibility. Even carrying around a pocket comb and a bottle of hairspray so you can touch up an actor's hair for a second take of a fight scene is part of the daily grind.

As with all the design departments, the hairdresser needs to know the period and be able to re-create it in a trailer on location. A lot of hairdressers are specifically requested by actors or directors they've worked with before. Loyalty counts. As in the real world, people will tell things to their hairdressers they won't tell anyone else. Just imagine what kinds of secrets the stars you work with might tell.

....................

## Food Stylist

The job of food stylist is not found often in feature films. Most work for food stylists is in stills or commercials, but every now and then a film job will require the specialized skills of somebody who can make camera-ready food. When that happens, one of the first people to get the call is Alice M. Hart, owner of Food for Film Stylists, a food stylist company.

What Alice does is prepare food to the manufacturer's specifications, making it look as good as possible. In a film, if the actors are eating something, it was probably prepared by craft service or the caterers. If it's a big banquet spread in the background of a scene, the prop department covered it. But if the camera comes in tight on specific pieces of food, then Alice comes in to create the perfect dish.

Commercials are where Alice is really put to the test, though. She starts working a week or two before the shoot, preparing the food and making kitchen arrangements.

Kitchens are their own headache, and Alice has had to convert empty soundstages to full-fledged gourmet kitchens. For a Taco Bell commercial, Alice took a cube truck (the kind normally used by the prop or camera departments), had a generator installed, and turned it into the most unusual kitchen on wheels ever seen.

Preparation, on the other hand, can make building kitchens seem like a walk in the park. Part of the preparation involves cooking the food as truly as possible. There are no sprays or dyes or shellacs here; everything is completely edible and made the same way you'd find it in the restaurant or out of the package. Since Alice has to make her food look as good as possible, she won't just grab a handful of her client's Trix cereal, dump it into a bowl, and shoot it. No, Alice will spend several days to a week going through dozens of boxes of Trix looking for the perfect, or "hero," pieces of cereal with which to fill her bowl. And not only one bowl. She may have to have four or five bowls ready at any point, depending on what the director wants. For a "milk drop," where milk is poured into the cereal, the cameras are filming at extraordinarily high speeds, up to 250 frames per second, with very hot lights. Under these conditions, the cereal may wilt or become damaged and need to be replaced every shot.

The other part of preparation is the shopping. Alice is a frequent visitor to her local supermarket at two o'clock in the morning, shopping for anything from a good piece of meat to the perfect chili pepper.

Sounds exciting, doesn't it? Alice loves it. She says there's never a dull moment. "But," she cautions, "it's not glamorous. It's grueling, dirty work. You can be on your feet for hours." Alice wouldn't do anything else.

Alice started her career as a chef for two years in Paris but says that most of the fifty or so people who work in the movie industry as food stylists have degrees in home economics. After getting out of college, a job with a food manufacturing company is the next step. Once involved with the food industry, hard work and determination will move you to where you want to be. As you advance, you should be acquiring pieces for your portfolio—stills of any print work you've done and a video reel of your film and commercial work. Or you can find someone like Alice to take you on as an apprentice. No matter how you go about getting into the field, Alice says the most important thing to know are these three words: *yes, I can.* Those words show you can be flexible and are a team player. And with all the people you're working with and for, diplomacy is something you can't afford to be without.

# For Further Information

Elias Root Beadle, a minister during the 1800s, wrote, "Half the work that is done in this world is to make things appear what they are not." For all we know, he could have been talking about the costume and makeup departments of any feature film, whose job it is to make things appear how the director wants them. If you enjoy this kind of playful subterfuge, the following books should give you a head start.

Buchman, Herman. *Stage Makeup*. New York: Watson-Guptil Publications.

Corson, Richard. *Stage Makeup, 9th Edition*. Boston: Allyn & Bacon.

Frank, Vivien, and Deborah Jaffe. *Making Masks*. Laguna Hills, CA: Walter Foster Publications.

James, Thurston. *The Prop Builder's Maskmaking Handbook*. Cincinnati, OH: F&W Publications.

La Motte, Richard. *Costume Design 101*. Studio City, CA: Michael Wiese Productions.

Place, Stan Campbell. *The Art and Science of Professional Makeup*. Clifton Park, NY: Milady Publishing.

# CHAPTER SEVEN

# Animation

## Drawing on Your Imagination

For kids throughout the country, Saturday mornings are the answer to weeklong prayers. It's got nothing to do with it being the end of the week or that there's no school or even that it is the first day of the weekend. It has to do with the cartoons on TV. And it's not just the kids who are getting excited.

Cartoons have been around for more than fifty years, and they are still going strong. The Walt Disney Company built an empire based on little flat images that look as if they are alive. Several of the longest-running prime-time shows on TV are animated. Why? What's the magic of animation?

The magic is that we believe it. When a real person gets hit in the head with an anvil or plummets thousands of feet over a cliff, we are appalled and disgusted. We hardly enjoy ourselves. But cartoons are different. Not only are we not disgusted, we giggle and guffaw.

## Voice Director

With animation, and this is how it differs from a regular film or TV show, actors are cast solely for the way their voices sound. Voice actors are cast through the same audition process as regular actors, but when it comes time to actually record the dialogue, they fall under the ear of the voice director. And if you can do more than one voice, even better; it gives you the chance to play more than one character.

The voice director sits in on the recording sessions to make sure the actors get the dialogue right. He or she will sometimes have the actor do a line several different ways to give the director something to choose from in case he or she wants to try something out of the ordinary.

## Animation Storyboard Artist

In Chapter 5, we discussed how storyboards are used for a regular feature. They're used much the same way here, only there are more of them. In a regular feature, a storyboard artist usually will not draw scenes with two characters sitting in a room talking. In animation, however, everything has to be boarded—everything—because nothing exists prior to this, and there is no way to just "improvise" a scene. The animators need to know what it is they are supposed to draw.

Animation storyboard artists do have an advantage over regular storyboarders: they have the sound track. In animation, all the voices are recorded prior to anything being drawn. Then the director and the storyboarders listen to the dialogue of the entire show and talk about how they want the show to look. Afterward, the storyboarders go to work.

As with live action, the animators need to know a bit about filmmaking. In fact, to do animation, the boarders need to know what can and can't be done within the sphere of animation. For instance, a live-action film can have a crane shot where everything, including the background, is in constant motion. The only way to do this in an animated film or TV show is to make extensive use of computers. A prime example of how this can work is the "jungle surfing" scenes in Disney's *Tarzan*, which employed a new technology known as Deep Canvas to make the backgrounds look more realistic than ever before.

Once the storyboards are drawn, anybody looking at them would be able to tell you what any of the characters was doing at any given moment. It's like an extremely detailed comic book of the whole show. This is good, because once the boards are done, the entire thing goes off to the designers.

## Animation Designer

Animation design really involves three different parts that make up the entire topic: backgrounds, characters, and props. Each is designed by a separate group of designers. On a feature film, these things are all designed once, at the beginning of the production, but on a weekly show like "The Simpsons," things have to be created for each episode.

If the script calls for something that has been seen before somewhere in the history of the show, the design is pulled and given to the animators and layout people, but if the writers have created something new, then it has to be designed from scratch.

Backgrounds are needed when a new setting is used. The designer creates what is the equivalent of a master shot, a view that encompasses the entire set, including everything called for in the script. If, for instance, the script called for a monorail cockpit, then the designer draws a straight-on view of the cockpit, showing all the dials and lights and details where they are supposed to be. The designer does one of these master shots for all new locations, and these are given to the background and layout artists for use during the next step.

At the start of a show or movie, all the characters are new, so they all have to be designed. In the case of a TV show, new characters appear each episode in the form of "guest stars" or just additions to help the story line along. The design of these characters is done in two steps. The first step is the actual drawing of the character from the front. This is the main look of the character, so it is the most important. Once the initial design is approved, the character undergoes a process called turnarounds. This is when an artist, usually someone who specializes in this procedure, takes the straight drawing and reproduces it several times. Each time, though, the artist changes the angle slightly—in effect, turns the body around, so when finished, the animator has a reference of what the character looks like from all sides. It's like watching a model spin on a runway. In fact, the sheet is used as a model, and all the animators must keep to it to ensure that the character's looks stay the same from scene to scene.

Prop design, as you've probably guessed, is the design of anything that is used by any of the characters. If there's a remote control being used to change a channel, that has to be designed by someone.

Once the model pack is approved, it is passed on to the animators whom the director has cast, or assigned, to the various aspects of the project.

## Animation Director

In animation, the director isn't dealing with actors. Here the job is a lot tougher—the director is dealing with drawings, pencil lines on flat pieces of paper. The only problem is, those drawings can be just as temperamental and difficult to work with as their real-life counterparts, and it's up to the director to keep them in line, so to speak.

Jeffrey Allen Lynch directs for the hit television show "The Simpsons." His job is to guide the episode through the steps to make it into a half-hour television show, but the steps are almost identical for an animated feature film. The first step is the storyboard, much like that for a regular feature, only more detailed. The storyboard then goes to the designers.

Once everything has been designed and approved by the director, all the characters, background, and prop models are bundled together into a "model pack" and given to the animators and background and layout artists. Everything that will appear in the show starts out its creative life here. In any animation studio, the model pack is referred to more often than the phone book.

Then it's time for the animation director to cast the show. Casting in animation is different from live-action casting. In the first place, all the voices have been hired and recorded already; we're not talking about them. Second, we already know what the characters look like since they were already designed. Then what does Jeffrey Lynch do to "cast" his show? He hands out assignments.

If a character is going to do a song and dance, then Jeffrey assigns that character to the animator he feels can do the best job. Usually, though, it's not that specific. Jeffrey knows which animator is good at which character and assigns accordingly. The same is true for backgrounds. Once Jeffrey hands out parts, it's time to animate and shoot.

## Character Layout Animator

Time for magic. Being an animator is the glory job in animation. It's also one of the hardest. Ask Dan Povenmire, who every week makes "The Simpsons" look alive.

Dan's job is to act out the action. He is really nothing more than an actor with a pencil. But we're not talking any type of Method here; we are talking about the key pose. We all know that animation is made up of thousands of single, static drawings that have been filmed to give the appearance of movement. Now the animator, especially on a weekly show or a feature, doesn't have the time to draw each frame—only the scenes where something changes, whether it's an expression, an emotion, or an action. These are the key poses, and this is where the acting comes in. A bad animator may not draw enough keys to properly convey the scene, and the performance of the animated character appears flat and lifeless. A good animator brings the character to life not only by doing enough key poses to show what's going on but also by adding little nuances, such as a bob of the head or a raised eyebrow, to give the performance the extra nudge needed to take it from the bland to the sublime.

Dan is a good animator, but then, he's been doing animation for a long time. He's had to learn the skills of his art the hard way, by trial and error, rather than by going to an art school. Not that learning on your own is the best way to go about it. Dan recommends art school, especially those that have animation programs, such as California Institute of the Arts or the Rhode Island School of Design. A lot of young animators are hired right out of schools like these. Tim Burton was. But if you don't want to go to school, here are some tips to help you learn.

Number one: draw.

Number two: draw a lot.

Number three: draw even more.

Draw things like flip books, which are series of drawings in corners of blank books or sketch pads, each one a little different, so that when the pages are rapidly turned, or flipped, it creates a basic animation. Dan used to create flip books in the corners of his school texts, but he doesn't recommend this, mostly because until you become famous, this does nothing for their resale value.

Another thing Dan did that he says helped him immeasurably was writing and drawing a comic strip, *Life As a Fish*, for his college newspaper. He says it taught him how to represent something in the least amount of lines.

When you're doing any type of animation and there's a deadline involved, knowing how to make something look like what you want it to look like in very little time, with as little detail as you can get away with, is a handy trick. Something that will help you to get a feel for drawing lines is reproducing other people's work. Learn how lines are used to construct and animate faces or hands—how, for example, by adding a little flourish to an eyebrow, you can make the character look happy or sad or angry. Once you can reproduce other people's work, throw it all away and create your own characters. You'll notice influences but, hopefully, the style you've developed will be uniquely your own.

Dan's last bit of advice: if someone will pay you to sit at a desk and doodle, and it's something you'd be doing anyway, you've got the makings of an animator. Now all you need is the initiative, and the work will be waiting for you.

# Background Layout Animator

If a character is walking along through the air, the audience probably won't buy it. Thus, we have discovered the need for backgrounds. Now, how does the job of doing backgrounds differ from the backgrounds created by the designer? Simple. For every shot in the cabin of the designer's monorail, the angle will be different, and the background must reflect that. The background artist, then, has to take the master shot design and extrapolate what the scene should look like from the side or looking up.

For Jeff "Swampy" Marsh, doing backgrounds (or BGs, as they're called in the industry) is all a matter of perspective. His experience prior to doing animation was three years of drafting classes in high school and college plus a bit of theater. This proved to be just the right combination because, as Swampy puts it, "The BG guys are just set builders for animation." They have to make the background look like what's happening in the scene.

Specifically, what Swampy does is take the key poses from the animator and, using the BG design and the storyboards for reference, draw the appropriate background. However, in some cases, the background is also the foreground. For that shot in the monorail cockpit, if the director wants to see a character's hands on the dashboard from the point of view of outside the front of the monorail, then the dashboard falls to the BGs. The general rule is that if it's not going to be animated, it's a background.

Swampy has to make sure the relative size is correct as well as the vanishing points and horizon lines, which is why his drafting background is important. If a vanishing point (a mythical point used for perspective drawings where everything would be unrecognizable and disappear into the distance) is wrong, then the entire sequence will look odd. Looking odd is not necessarily bad, but if the viewers think something is wrong but can't figure out exactly what, it will nag at them, destroying the mood and credibility that directors like Jeffrey Lynch strive so hard to build.

Swampy's library consists of several dozen art books as well as shelves of architecture design and rendering books, and he is constantly referring to them to make sure he gets it right. BGs might not be as glamorous as actual animators, but they are just as important.

...............

# Timer

Barring unforeseen complications, all the key poses and BGs have been turned in to director Jeffrey Lynch and checked over by Howard Parkins, an assistant director. It's time to shoot.

No matter how great a job the animators have done, everything needs to come together under the camera. That's where Pete Michels shows his stuff. Pete is an animation timer. His job is crucial to making everything come out okay.

To do his job well, Pete has to know about how animation, as well as an animation camera, works. He has to be able to use tools such as field guides and stopwatches. He has to know that the camera shoots two frames for every drawing. He has to write out the instructions of what to do with the art.

Pete takes the audio tape of the dialogue, the storyboards, and the key poses and writes them out on an exposure, or "X," sheet. This sheet shows how the dialogue breaks down (by syllables) and where in each line the keys are drawn. It tells the camera what should be "exposed" on each frame. The timer has to decide how many frames it will take to get from one key to the next. Pete is instrumental in determining pacing. If the scene is supposed to be slow, Pete can add time. If the scene is quick, Pete can take time away or add movement within the scene to give it a sense of drama. The little stuff also falls under Pete's jurisdiction. If two characters are conversing in a scene (which could be extremely boring in an animated piece), the one talking is getting all the action. Pete compensates and adds ancillary motions, such as eye blinks, that keep the other characters from being static images.

Like Mozart, who could compose without listening to music, Pete has to animate without actually animating. He has to know what it's going to look like and write that on the X sheet. Each character, as well as each background, is animated on a different level of film, and Pete has to make sure all of the levels will work together before he sends it off to the camera department to shoot the sequence.

The first time the sequence is shot, it's called an animatic, and it is the equivalent of dailies or a rough cut in live action. The animatic is also referred to as a pencil test; it is a rough look at what the finished product will look like without color and without a lot of the ancillary action. It looks a lot like a filmed comic book, with the key poses taking up as much screen time as it takes to get to the next one.

Once the animatic is delivered, Jeffrey, Pete, and Howard all watch it with the producers and the writers. They fix anything that doesn't work and completely redo anything brand new. Otherwise, that's it for the animatic. Usually, there is only enough time and money to do it once. If anything really complicated needs to be shot before the final is finished, it will be done on videotape.

## In-Betweener or Assistant Animator

The in-betweener animates the stuff in between the key poses. It sounds pretty self-explanatory, and it is. The in-betweener animates sequences such as walk cycles, where all the character is doing is walking. On a TV show like "The Simpsons," all the in-between work is done at animation studios overseas, in countries such as Korea, Japan, or Russia. On a feature film, though, the assistant animator is in the next cubicle and has a good working relationship with the animator. The animator knows how much to draw to get the message across and may even let the assistant animator draw some minor sequences to get the experience needed to become an animator.

The in-betweener also cleans up the drawings of the animator, if needed, tightening up the lines, darkening the shadows, and so forth.

...............................

## Color Designer

All of the drawings are done, the animation is working, and the director is pleased. The only problem is that it's all in black and white. There's no color. Better send everything down to the ink and paint department.

Everything in an animated world has its own color, and those colors should work together to create a visually pleasing whole. In other words, make sure the shirt and the sky aren't the same, or you'll never see one against the other.

Carol Wyatt's job is just that. She gets to spend her days coloring, and as long as she stays within the lines, everything's alright.

As a designer, Carol takes a background design, photocopies it onto a clear piece of acetate, called a cell, and paints it, using colors at her discretion. Since Carol has a background with color skills and theory, her discretion is usually trusted. Once a BG design is colored, the director and producers have approval. If they don't like it, Carol has to go back and do it again. At up to eight hours for a complicated BG, you can see how this could get old real quick.

When she started the ink and paint department on "The Simpsons," Carol instituted a computer color design system. The BGs still have to be painted by hand, but the higher brass could see several different samples on the screen from which to make a choice. "The Simpsons" was the first TV series to use a computer system like this.

The same process is used for characters and props. Each design is scanned into the computer and colored. Once it is approved, the design is hand painted by cell painters. The finished paintings are called color keys.

Most animated feature films are now done this way as well, including both Disney's film *Lilo & Stitch* and Fox's *Ice Age*. This is why there were no cells produced for those films. All the backgrounds and animation were scanned in, painted electronically, and output directly to 35 mm film for editing.

## Colorist

Each production has a set of colors used throughout the run of the show. For each of these hundreds of colors, a number is assigned. The colorists have the job of assigning these colors to the drawings. They take the keys from the designers and fill in the corresponding numbers on the backgrounds from the BG artists. Then what gets sent overseas is a collection of paint-by-number cells.

This isn't as easy as it sounds. If the scene is in a living room, it will probably follow the key pretty closely. But what happens if the power suddenly goes out and the living room is thrown into darkness? The only light is coming from the moon shining in the window. There won't be another key created for "moonlit living room," so the colorists have to figure out what those key colors would look like in the dark, then put those numbers where the colors are supposed to go.

## Assistant Director

Assistant director Howard Parkins functions much like his live-action counterpart. He is on the show from the beginning, and part of his job is to look at all the artwork as it comes in and double-check it for continuity, modeling, and size relations.

Howard is always ready to fill any role the director may require of him, even to the point of directing smaller sequences. In many ways, he is a director-in-training, and he's had to climb up through the ranks to get there. He started with art school in Canada and found a job as an assistant animator on a feature film right after graduation. Then, after a stint in London as a cell painter, Howard did in-betweens for *Who Framed Roger Rabbit?* His animation has taken him all over the world, and he knows that as long as he can draw or paint, he's got a passport to anywhere.

## Creating Your Portfolio

Animation portfolios should contain a different kind of art sample than a regular portfolio. Sure, a director like Jeffrey Lynch wants to see your fully rendered life drawings (for a character animator) or nicely detailed landscape paintings (for a background artist), but what he wants to see even more are your quick pen sketches—anything that can show him body language, acting. In animation, every picture must literally tell a story. Your portfolio should show that you can draw those kinds of pictures, and do it quickly.

Being able to capture weight, emotion, and attitude in either human or animal characters is a plus. Bring your sketchbook because a director will probably want to see it. And don't be afraid of not having people who look just like people. It's okay, maybe even preferred, to be a bit "cartoony." After all, this is animation, and th-th-th-that's all, folks.

## For Further Information

The cartoon world is calling out to new talent. The following books and organizations will help you prepare to answer that call.

### Books

Gray, Milton. *Cartoon Animation—Introduction to a Career.* Northridge, CA: Lion's Den Publications.

Laybourne, Kit. *The Animation Book.* New York: Three Rivers Press.

Levitan, Eli L. *Handbook of Animation Techniques.* New York: Van Nostrand Reinhold.

Maestri, George. *Character Animation 2: Essential Techniques.* Indianapolis: New Riders Publishing.

Pintoff, Ernest. *Animation 101.* Studio City, CA: Michael Wiese Productions.

Weishar, Peter. *Blue Sky: The Art of Computer Animation.* New York: Harry N. Abrams Books.

Whitaker, Harold. *Timing for Animation.* Burlington, MA: Elsevier Science/Harcourt.

White, Tony. *The Animator's Work Book.* New York: Watson-Guptill Publications.

## Organizations and Schools

American Animation Institute
The Animation Guild
4729 Lankershim Boulevard
North Hollywood, CA 91602
http://mpsc839.org


Cartoon Colour
9024 Lindblade Street
Culver City, CA 90232
www.cartooncolor.com
   *(Mail-order animation supply house.)*


Harvard University Animation School
Department of Visual and Environmental Studies
24 Quincy Street
Cambridge, MA 02138
www.ves.fas.harvard.edu

# Special Effects

## Lifelike...Only More So

D o you remember how you felt the first time you saw *Star Wars*? The excitement of watching the introductory words scroll up from the bottom of the screen, then instead of going straight up and off the top, recede into the distance. Then along came the massive spaceship, the *Imperial Star Cruiser*, ominously filling the frame in hot pursuit of the rebel ship, blue lasers firing into the star-filled blackness of space—a huge battle for freedom taking place a long time form now in a galaxy far, far away. In reality, you saw a couple of models shot against a blue screen in a warehouse, with the lasers scratched in later. Either way, the magic was there. A modern force in special effects had been born.

*Star Wars* was far from the beginning. Special effects have been around since 1901, but it was not until the huge box-office success of films like *Star Wars* and *Close Encounters of the Third Kind*, both released in 1977, that science fiction was taken seriously as a film genre and the special effects predominant in such films were considered important. Since then, the special effects field has become one of the fastest-growing fields in the entire film industry. There are dozens of companies, or shops, ready to bring a writer's or director's vision to life. And all of them have to be constantly on the lookout for new people, the fresh blood that will bring new perspectives to the field. The shop with the best innovations wins the contract to do the next Spielberg film.

Of course, there are many different kinds of effects, with just as many shops to handle them. Depending on your talents and interests, you could find a place with any one of them. Some of these include:

Puppetry
Creature effects
Computer effects or computer graphic images (CGI)
Makeup effects
Animation effects
Pyrotechnics
Miniatures
Mattes

Each of these facets of the effects field has its own guidelines and required skills. How do you decide which one is best for you? Focus on your abilities and put them where they would be most useful.

## Puppetry

When someone starts talking about puppets, the first image that comes to this author's mind is Kermit the Frog. Kermit, technically, is not really a puppet, but a muppet, which is basically a sock with someone's hand manipulating the mouth and some rods controlling the arms. And that comprises the common perception of puppets and puppeteering: a sock and a hand.

However, with today's technology, puppeteering has become much more. You can now get a degree in puppetry from some colleges, and, very often, your hand is not even in physical contact with the puppet whose features you are controlling.

Even if your hand (or hands, yours and others) is right up in the thick of the action, the puppet you're operating no longer resembles anything like a sock. More likely, it's a carefully sculpted piece of foam latex filled with electronics that enable it to blink or furrow its brow.

Under the heading of puppetry, you will find diverse job descriptions requiring a multitude of talents and utilizing everything from one finger to your entire body.

## Suit Performer

If you want to use your entire body, this is the area of puppeteering you want to be in. Technically, the suit performer is considered an actor. That is, he or she brings the physical movement of the character to life.

Suit performers are something of a different breed. They can range anywhere from walking around in a Godzilla suit on a miniature set to lurking in the shadows waiting to fight Sigourney Weaver in the *Alien* films. A suit performer for film or television has to create the physical carriage of the character, how it walks, stands, sits. It's acting without words. If the scene requires the character to be sad, the suit performer has to show that through the layers of the costume. Here the suit performer is not working alone. The costume has any number of electronic controls operating the face and any other part of the creation that needs extra articulation. These controls are operated by a second or even third person. The operator of these extra functions is in constant communication with the suit performer, working in harmony to create the perfect performance necessary for the shot.

"Before my audition, I videotaped myself walking around my apartment, eating breakfast, dancing, like a dinosaur." This is what suit performer Bill Barretta did to prepare for the role of Earl in Disney Television's show "Dinosaurs." Bill is an actor who finds being literally inside a character a challenge. "From training in movement, you learn to have a certain balance and how to move and how to create certain things. Most of my acting is based on behavior, which is really what I do." Bill has to be able to interpret the script as a whole, not just for his character. "I have to be able to figure out what the behavior is that will tell the story without really having to hear the words.

"Every time I get a script, I go through it, and as I'm reading it there are things that I just imagine [the character] doing. There are always ideas that I'm coming up with." In this way, Bill, like any actor, has input into the creation of the personality of his character.

Other aspects of the job? "Just being creative and open to suggestions and collaboration are a big part of what we do. It's good to have an open mind. You have so many people who work on the show, [giving ideas]. If you close yourself off to that sort of stuff, you're losing rather than gaining."

## Electronic Puppeteer

In the modern world of filmmaking, there are all sorts of things you need to know in order to make a creature come to life. A suit performer needs to rely on someone like Steve Whitmire to help realize a character. Steve operates the facial aspects on a walk-around suit. While he continues to do hand puppetry (he is the hands and voice behind Kermit the Frog), the other aspect of his job requires much more in the way of a technical background. Steve has to be able to program a computer. This computer is wired to his controller and tells the puppet what to do. If he wants it to smile, he simply does a preprogrammed move or hits a pre-programmed toggle combination and he gets the reaction he wants. "The only way to learn is to be doing it, to be on the floor or in a film or on television doing this stuff. The best way to rehearse is in front of a video camera, not in front of a mirror— it's different; it's backwards."

Steve began puppeteering as a kid, building his own puppets and performing with them. "The real interest for me has been in knowing how they work and building them," he says. He has spent hours in front of video cameras, practicing, getting his craft down. He is always trying to develop new characters he can use. "There's more involved in developing new characters than there is in continuing the technical side of learning puppetry." In the course of his career, not only have his puppets graced film and television screens, but he even had a chance to introduce one of his favorite bands, the rock group Kansas, at one of its concerts.

## Hand Puppeteer

The other half of modern puppetry is the old hand puppet. Puppeteer Kevin Clash is one of the best; he has even won an Emmy Award for his work on "Sesame Street," where he plays Elmo. He has his hands right in the thick of things, manually controlling all the facial reactions and expressions of his puppet, especially the mouth.

But even Kevin rarely works alone. Even with the simplest of muppets, there is usually at least one other person operating the hands.

Most of the Henson puppeteers do their own voices, and Kevin suggests developing five really strong ones. Those voices can then be applied or modified to fit any character you're given to do. And if a new voice comes to you, use it, nurture it, and add it to your repertoire. "It's a great job—you can act as crazy as you want."

## Getting Started in Puppetry

If you want to work with the Henson company, it holds puppeteering workshops and auditions throughout the year. Contact the company for information; the address is listed at the end of this chapter. If you tape yourself playing with your puppets, send the tape to the Henson Company. That's where you start, but Steve Whitmire warns: "We look for people who are not afraid to be really stupid, really silly, and who have no problem in going over the top."

## Creature Effects

Let's take a look at *Men in Black* for a minute—specifically, the first time Agent J sees inside MIB headquarters. Remember all those creatures? The aliens no one on Earth had ever dreamed of?

Well, somebody must have dreamed of them at some point because they were created and filmed.

All the aliens, mutants, gremlins, or critters ever seen in the movies were built by a creature shop. Whether it was one person working alone in a garage or the Jim Henson shop in London, they all had the same goal: to come up with something no one else had ever seen.

To get to this point, the first thing that had to happen was the creatures had to be designed.

## Creature Designer

In film, all things start with the story. From there, the story is turned into a script, and then all the creative people get hold of it. If the film calls for a creature of some sort, then one of the first people to get a look at the script is the creature designer. The creature designer reads the description the author wrote, which can be anything ranging from a detailed passage to simply "a scary monster," sees how the creature must react within the story, and designs something that will encompass it all.

Kirk Thatcher, who is now a producer, spent a lot of time in creature design. When Kirk designs, he takes ideas from everywhere, from all the books he's read or the pictures he's seen. He tries to design creatures that give away the character by appearance alone. If the creature is supposed to be lovable, it should be lovable from the first time it is seen on screen. The same holds true if it's scary.

To be a creature designer, you should have a background that includes some sort of art training. This training should not be limited to just drawing but should include all the fine arts, and if you add in some mechanical background, it can only help. But don't expect to start as a creature designer. It's a position you work up to, mainly by doing it. Build creatures of your own and learn the process. Put your creations into a portfolio and use it to sell your work.

## The Next Step

It used to be that after someone like Kirk finished the design, and it was approved by the director, it would be sent off to the shop where it would be sculpted, cast, painted, fabricated, and mechanized, roughly in that order. It still happens that way for a number of creatures; that scene we were talking about in *MIB*, for example. But in a growing number of cases, those creatures never exist outside of a computer terminal. And for those creatures, a whole different set of skills is required.

We'll talk about the physical creatures first.

## Sculptor

The designer has just handed over the final sketches, and it's up to you, the sculptor, to make them three-dimensional. You get to use specialized tools and create in clay your interpretation of the creature asked for.

The sculptor is important because it is this artist's work, ultimately, that ends up on the screen. What the final product is intended to be determines how the project is done. If you are going to be sculpting a large hand puppet without much facial activity, you may need to do just some basic foam carving.

Small creatures are much more detailed and are usually sculpted out of clay. Since they range anywhere from several inches to three feet or more in height, the sculptor usually uses some sort of skeleton or armature in the approximate shape of the creature on which to anchor the sculpture, then builds the clay up around that.

If your task is the full-size body suit for some alien from a distant galaxy, then your methods will be slightly different. What you'll be doing is sculpting a clay skin, lighter in specific details but more accurate in the details you do choose to show. You'll still use clay, only a lot more of it. Your internal support could be anything from a cardboard mock-up to a fiberglass cast shell taken from the performer who will be wearing the suit.

## Mold Maker

How does a creature go from being a stiff, clay sculpture to a seemingly living, breathing monster? It makes a stop at the mold maker's station. Here, the clay creation is cast in plaster (or some other casting agent) to create a negative mold. The mold maker has to decide how many pieces the mold needs to be and how those pieces are to be split, taking into consideration all the nooks and crannies of the original design.

Next, the mold maker casts the creature in sections, blocking the various parts of the sculpture by building retaining walls of clay to prevent the plaster from getting into those areas. Usually a mold maker inserts a marble or some other type of imperfection into a side, which has to be matched to another side to be cast later. Then, as both sides are cast, one has a marble sticking out and the other has an indentation where the marble will rest comfortably. This is the only way these two pieces can possibly fit together. By the time the mold is completed, there is only one way all the pieces can join seamlessly. The mold maker has then completed this part of the creature assembly line and passes the contribution along.

## Foam Latex Runner

The foam runner takes the negative molds and turns them into positive creations. What the foam runner is responsible for is mixing the foam latex (or whatever it is the creature is going to be cast in) to the correct consistency, then pouring it into the mold, making sure it is the correct thickness. If it is too thick, the creature will not be able to move correctly; if it is too thin, it will rip and tear easily, making it useless after a couple of takes. If the creature is an integral part of the film, the latex runner will probably end up making several copies of the creature, either whole or just certain articulated parts that will get more use than the others.

The nice thing about being a foam latex runner is that it is a job not many people want to do, making it easier to break into the industry by doing it. If you can learn quickly how to mix and pour the various elements you'll be working with or, even better, play with latex at home and learn about it, finding a break-in job should be no problem.

## Scumbler

This is it: the premiere, bottom-of-the-ladder, entry-level special effects job. Sometimes it's associated with latex running or even mold making, depending on the size of the shop you work for, but with the exception of being a production assistant (as described in Chapter 2), this is your way in the door.

The scumbler takes the rough latex creation and, before passing it along to the painter, cleans it up. Primarily, this means getting rid of the seams. A seam is formed everywhere two pieces of the mold fit together. You can see them on any small plastic toy you buy. Somewhere around the edges you'll see a thin line, which may be perfectly smooth or may be slightly raised. The stuff cleaned off of a seam to make it smooth is called scumble, hence the job title of scumbler.

While you're scumbling, you also have to remove the latex that is filling in the eye holes, the mouth, and any other orifice that has been filled in during the casting process and needs to be cleared. From here it's just a short hop into a dedicated creature effects position.

## Painter

Okay, the creature is all cleaned up and ready for a night on the set, right? Not quite yet. Right now, your creature (which by this point in any production would have a name so that the people in the shop would have some way to refer to it; we'll call it Spot) looks like a single-color lump. Whatever color the latex was to begin with, Spot is completely that color. If Spot were to be shown against a black background, then being all white would be okay, but odds are, your director will want Spot to have some sort of definition. That's why the sculptor put so much effort into all the detail. The only way to give Spot this detail is to paint it.

So, as a painter, you go back to the original sketches made by the designer to see what kind of color scheme Spot should have. Here's where a strong art background comes in. Spot is going to need to be painted in a variety of shades and colors. You are going to need to be able to use everything from a fine, camel hair, two-bristle brush to a paint roller to an airbrush. You will have to know about shading and blending, and you may also be responsible for putting in two-dimensional details such as veins or laugh lines. You may even want to learn a bit about musculature in case you need to know where creases should occur if Spot were going for a walk or raising its arms.

## Fabricator

Spot is almost ready for the limelight. The creature looks good, but it's bald, has no eyes or teeth, and resembles something you'd see in an intergalactic prison, with a tattoo reading "Mother" in an alien language. Since the director has probably specified Spot to have hair, eyes, and teeth, we'd better give it some.

If Spot's eyes are going to move, they'll be added as part of the mechanics, which we'll get to in a moment. But if not, they'll be added here. Eyes are usually made out of some sort of plastic or glass and cast or ground to fit the holes the sculptor has left. The eyes are then attached to Spot's skull by either glue or stitching.

Next come the teeth. Depending on what Spot's teeth have to do, they will be sculpted from soft materials, such as cast foam, or hard materials, such as dental resin.

Spot's hair, however, is a job all on its own. Putting in hair is a highly specialized task called hair punching, and it involves affixing each individual strand of hair one at a time. Jennie Wanniski has spent a lot of time punching hair. "It's very time consuming," she says. "You have to have a great amount of patience and be a perfectionist." Jennie also suggests a sewing background is helpful, although not necessary: "If you know how to tie things off, it can't hurt."

Fabricators also have the task of joining all of Spot's various parts together. If the arms and legs were cast separately, then the fabricator has to put them together. By the time the fabricator's work is done, Spot is all one creature.

## Mechanic

Spot is now ready to face the footlights. Our creature looks really good, but he can't move much. Time for the mechanics to work their magic: creating a musculature for Spot, something to hang the nice, finished skin on. Most times, the mechanics focus on the face and head because this is where the most movement and expression take place. They might put controls in the limbs (and tail, if Spot has one) so outside operators can move them, but these controls are relatively simple—back and forth, up and down—compared to creating complex facial expressions with wires and cables.

As a mechanic, you'll take a rough cast of the latex skin and build a fiberglass skull based on its dimensions. You have to take things such as eye sockets and lips into account. When you're done with Spot, it not only has to be able to do all the things required by the script, such as smile viciously or frown scornfully, but also display a host of other expressions the director might call for. During the filming of the 1988 remake of the horror film *The Blob*, the director asked that the Blob (whom the effects crew called Irving) look down the street "menacingly." For something that had no face and nothing to distinguish front from back, this was no easy task. But the effects crew members did their best to make it happen. Using only their hands underneath slime-covered silk, the "blob-ateers" would make harsh, jerky movements to convey anger and menace.

The mechanic is the effects industry's tinkerer, the one who wants to know how all the different gadgets and doodads work. In addition to being able to machine needed parts, the mechanic should know how to put them together. He or she needs to be able to analyze things like the differences between using hydraulics or compressed air. A good mechanic is able to take the creature designs and create from them a mechanical schematic that includes all of the hardware and connectors needed.

If Spot is going to be run by computers and electronics as well as manual operation, the mechanic also needs to work with the electronic effects people to make sure everything is compatible.

## Computer Graphic Images (CGI)

Welcome to the new millennium. Nearly every film that comes out of a major studio or high-profile independent company uses some sort of CGI somewhere. Whether it's big and obvious—such as putting Tom Hanks in the same shot as John F. Kennedy in *Forrest Gump*, adding tigers to the arena in the Academy Award–winning *Gladiator*, or even sinking the *Titanic*—or small and subtle, such as changing the color of the sky or the type of plane being flown in the finale of *Independence Day*, computer effects are here to stay. But how do you get involved? Let's take a look.

### Input/Output (I/O) Operator

The input/output person at an effects house is one step up from a production assistant (unless there's no PA, in which case you might have to get the coffee as well). I/O people are the record keepers and the organizers. Using computers, the I/O staff is responsible for logging and categorizing everything that comes into the shop. They'll create databases for every effects shot, letting the compositors know how many frames they have to work with, and keep track of the progress being made for each shot.

When a movie such as *Spy Kids 2: The Island of Lost Dreams* has more than a thousand different effects, that's a lot to keep track of. If you have a good knowledge of UNIX and a mind that can focus on small details, then this may be the perfect place for you to break in.

## Scanner/Recorder

When a piece of film comes in, after it's been logged, it somehow needs to be translated to a digital medium so it can be manipulated. That's the job of the scanner/recorder.

Working in a *clean room*, that is to say one where you have to wear lab coats and walk across a sticky mat to make sure you don't track *any* dirt inside, you take the negative and scan it into the computer. This is done frame by frame at an incredibly high resolution so the computer can capture every nuance of light and color recorded by the director of photography.

Once the frames are scanned, they are coded by shot number in the computer, where anyone who needs to find them, can. Remember, for a ten-second scene, that can mean as many as 240 frames.

Then the magic happens.

Once the animators and compositors have had their way with the frame, it needs to come back out of the computer so we can see it at our local multiplex.

Again, the scanner/recorder steps up, this time wearing the recorder part of the hat. He or she takes the completed frame and, using a specialized camera, shoots it onto a single frame of film. When each sequence is done, it is sent to the lab and then to the director for approval.

Then the process starts over with the next shot (unless, of course, reshoots are needed).

## Programmer

You don't really need to know anything at all about film to land a job as a programmer, but it couldn't hurt. Here you're designing the software and controls that let the rest of the team create the most lifelike creature or environment they can.

A background in C++, a knowledge of the software currently available, and a general love of tinkering in code will certainly get you "logged on" for this type of work.

## Animator

Once the character or creature has been designed, the animator is the one to bring it to life. While similar to the animator described in Chapter 7, a CGI animator does things slightly differently.

The CGI animator is responsible for every movement. Once the character has been imported into the computer, the animator starts the process by using what's called a wire frame of the creature. This is a rough approximation of how the final creature will look, with all the grid lines mapped out. The wire frame allows the animator to see how everything attaches together.

This becomes very important because unlike traditional animation, in CGI when you move one part of the body, the computer automatically moves other parts. Now it's up to the animator to make sure they're all moving correctly.

For a known creature, say a lion or elephant, as in *Jumanji*, the animator observes the animal as much as possible, either through films or field trips to the zoo or, in some cases, having the animal brought to the studio. When the creature is an alien life form, such as Jar Jar Binks in *Star Wars* episodes I and II, then it's up to the animators and director to figure out how it would move.

With all that established, the animators start to work. They create key frames and then allow the computer to fill in the rest. This process isn't as easy as it sounds, though. Since the demands are for computer-generated creations to look more and more lifelike, the animators must carefully detail every little bit of movement, creating separate key frames for different body parts, since they don't all move at the same speed or at the same time.

## Modeler

Once the animators are done, or even while they're still finishing up, the modeler comes in and brings lifelike touches such as skin and hair to the creation. The modeler sometimes even has to worry about clothes. For *Stuart Little 2*, the modeler worked with the costume designer to make sure the mouse was dressed appropriately.

In addition to characters, modelers are also responsible for CGI backgrounds. If the film's sets are computer generated, then the modelers must add the details, such as tapestries on the walls of a palace or the soot and grime of a derelict spaceship.

A background in art is essential here, as well as knowing computer painting software. When you're blending pixels on your palette, knowing as much as you can about the way things look in real life will help you re-create them on the computer.

## Compositor

Compositing is where it all comes together. This is where the creatures and the backgrounds and the live action are all mixed together to give the audience the sense of a seamless scene.

Because everything is in the computer, it seems as if all the compositor does is grab all the elements and slap them together like a jigsaw puzzle, but that's not entirely accurate. A jigsaw puzzle can go together only one way, while a scene can be composited any number of ways. The compositor needs to be able to judge density, size, and contrast to make sure things that are supposed to look far away, do. He or she also makes sure items created in the computer don't pass through real items, such as walls or people.

There's also a huge sense of timing that goes along with compositing. When you're adding in an explosion, you have to add it at exactly the right frame; otherwise it will look fake. If it's done, right, though, it can look perfect. For a low-budget film, the effects team of Howard/Granite used a still picture of a city, some overhead shots of cars moving, and a couple of explosions to create a composite of an end-of-the-world scenario. They put moving cars on the streets to give it a sense of action and then set off the explosions, smaller in the distance and larger as they got closer. In all, they completely destroyed a major metropolitan area for little money, lots of time, and no actual damage.

Compositors can also do subtle things such as change backgrounds, add shadows (remember the spaceship's approach in *Independence Day?*), even combine two live-action elements (the tiger scene in *Gladiator* is a prime example—the big cats were nowhere near the actors).

If this sounds like fun, manipulating time and space to get the ultimate, perfect scene, then by starting in I/O, you might just end up putting yourself in the picture.

## Stop-Motion Animation

Stop-motion animation takes the complete creature, sculpted and cast body and skeleton, and animates it. Animation is a long process that requires terrific amounts of patience. With stop motion, the creature is posed, and a single frame of film is exposed. Then the animator steps in and moves the creature a fraction of whatever the whole motion is and exposes another frame. Since there are twenty-four frames in a second of film, a several-minute segment (see *The Golden Voyage of Sinbad* or *King Kong* for examples of some of the best) may have as many as seventy-two hundred or more individual moves and take weeks to complete.

For argument's sake, let's say Spot is a fully articulated creature created to be sent off to a miniature set and, without the aid of puppeteers, expected to come to life. Stop motion would definitely be the way to go.

All of the design and most of the fabrication would follow the same lines as for any other creature, up to a point. The differences occur with the mechanics, who now have to build an actual skeleton for the creature. This skeleton can be made of anything from simple wood dowels (for low-budget films, home movies, or demo reels) to elaborate ball-and-socket metal armatures hand machined specifically for the project. Either way, the skeletons do the job of keeping Spot from moving between each take.

### Claymation Animator

Claymation is the same as stop motion only instead of fabricating the creatures out of latex and foam and making them posable, the creations are made of clay and have to be resculpted for each successive shot. Short films such as the Wallace and Grommit series and films like *Chicken Run* are created this way. The multiple award–winning *Chicken Run* is only the second full-length feature to be done completely in claymation (the first was *The Adventures of Mark Twain*). At eighty-four minutes, *Chicken Run* required more than 124,000 frames to be shot.

## Makeup Effects

Makeup effects are quite similar to creature effects with the exception that they are usually designed to fit over some part of an actor's anatomy. While a creature suit may be designed to be worn by a performer, makeup is applied directly to the actor. A lot of the steps are the same, though, along with the addition of some new ones. For this example, we will assume the makeup is being done to the actor's face, although the same steps apply to whatever is being made up.

There are two types of makeup: two-dimensional and three-dimensional. Two-dimensional, or flat, makeup is exactly what it sounds like. These are the effects done solely with color and shading. Creating a bruise is a perfect example of flat makeup. If you get into the makeup effects field in any capacity, you should have at least a working knowledge of two-dimensional makeup. Even beauty makeup is helpful, which we talked about in more detail in Chapter 6.

Three-dimensional makeup is what is commonly meant when someone talks about special effects makeup, and it refers to the creation of something that will rise off the actor's skin, ranging from a scar or a gunshot wound to having the actor transform into a werewolf right in front of the camera.

### Makeup Designer

The makeup designer's job is to make somebody look different than she or he really looks. All designs are based on the requirement that the makeup has to fit an actor. Also taken into account is the time the actor will have to spend having the makeup reapplied every day of the shoot, as opposed to a creature, which can be put on and taken off as easily as a rubber mask. The application can take a long time. To turn Jim Carrey into the Grinch required hours of sitting in a chair every morning before the rest of the crew showed up.

The same type of skills apply to makeup design as to creature design, although most makeup artists will actually sculpt their makeup creations themselves as opposed to having someone else do it. This is a general rule and doesn't hold true for all shops.

## Face Caster

The job of a face caster is to create the plaster mold on which the makeup will be sculpted. This mold is a lifelike replica of the actor's face and is used in the same way the skeleton is used in creature work. A face caster prepares the actor for the casting process and verbally guides him or her through it. One note of caution: please don't try this at home.

Once you have the actor in the chair, you cover the person's hair with a bald cap and mark off where the hair line is. Then things get extremely fun.

Next, you cover the face with a goopy solution called alginate, which hardens into a rubbery solid. Alginate is normally used by orthodontists to cast teeth, and special effects people picked up on it because of its wonderful ability to capture all the details of whatever it's poured over. It's kind of like when your fingerprints end up in a lump of clay.

Once the alginate has completely covered the actor, you cover the alginate with strips of plaster. If you didn't, the alginate would not be able to hold any shape, and it would collapse in on itself, becoming useless. The plaster strips provide a shell for the alginate to rest in.

After the plaster has dried, the entire negative can be removed, carefully, from the actor's head. A quick cleanup of the mold, and you're ready to make the positive. Just pour in some quick-set plaster, and in a few short hours, you've got a head, which, if you've done it right, should look like a bald twin of the actor. Now take your head, called a life cast, over to the sculptor.

From this point, makeup effects follow the same pattern as creature effects, until the makeup is delivered. Then there is one additional job.

## Makeup Applicator

If you love special effects and you want to work with celebrities, this is the job for you. The applicator takes all the sculpted pieces of latex, called appliances, that have been created from the actor's life cast and attaches them to the actor. The appliances are the special effect additions to the actor's face that were created by the sculptor and are applied using spirit gum or some other nontoxic adhesive. Makeup is used to blend the color to match with the actor's face so the camera can't tell where one stops and the other begins.

You must have a feel for colors and shadings, as well as a large amount of patience, for this job. When the actor is sitting in the chair for hours every day, you are right there conversing, making him or her feel at ease while you're gluing on laser burns or cybernetic features. A background in regular makeup might also prove beneficial when it comes time to do the actual blending.

## Effects Animator

Effects animators create the added touches that elevate things from ordinary to brilliant. Unlike regular animators, whose job is to bring characters to life, effects animators are more background players. They are the detail people. You may not notice their work, but if it weren't there, you would certainly miss it.

Effects animators are responsible for features such as lightning or electrical sparks. In every Steven Spielberg film where a shooting star is seen flashing through the night sky, it was done by an effects animator.

Another example of this work would be the sparkles that gleam from teeth in toothpaste commercials.

## Pyrotechnicians

When you see that shot of the huge fireball exploding out of the supposedly deserted mine shaft the heroes just went into, you know the pyrotechnicians had their hands in it. Any explosion, detonation, blast, or barrage is the domain of the pyrotechnic.

The pyrotechnicians just love to make things go boom. And even though they may seem a little crazy, the job requires them to be completely sane—and fully certified by the state as pyrotechnic operators.

## Miniature Modeler

Let's face it, if the script calls for a spaceship a mile long, it would be impractical to actually build the thing. You wouldn't be able to find a studio space big enough to store it, and even if you could, the odds of finding a studio big enough to afford it are even slimmer. For that matter, it's not very cost efficient to blow up things like jetliners or helicopters either. But what do you do? If the script calls for these things, somebody has to be responsible for making it happen. You can't expect the writer or director to change the movie just because something like a mile-long spaceship doesn't exist. The first thing to do is to make it exist. That's where David M. Jones comes in.

David creates things that don't exist or replicates things that do in order to do things to them that couldn't be done in real life. Such is the world of miniatures. However, the world of miniatures also encompasses special effects props.

David has been making models since he was a kid. Since he always wanted to fly, he started building his own jet planes from prefabricated kits. Then, after four years in design school, he was ready for the big time. But he never stopped building things. He thinks that besides actual model-making ability, the ability to draw, to sketch out your ideas quickly and accurately for the director, is of paramount importance. It saves a lot of time if you can illustrate a design rather than having to build it.

Once the design is approved, then the model-building skills come into play. According to David, the best builders are the ones who love doing this sort of stuff. These are the kids who grew up building models from kits, then when the kits were no longer a challenge, started building things from scratch. Also, the builders who know how to use industrial equipment, such as mills or the lathe, are the ones who have taken the passion from a mere hobby to something that could lead to a career. And there is a career out there for those who have all these skills.

Before you start working professionally (and sometimes after), you have to do everything yourself. "Sometimes," David says, "you're more of a technician than an artist." You should be able to draw your idea, draft it to figure out how to build it, design working prototypes, and, finally, build a finished product and photograph it so it can rest in your portfolio. It is this portfolio you'll take with you on interviews when you're trying to find work.

An experienced modeler like David can tell, from a glance at pictures of your finished work, what kind of a model maker you are. He can tell if you have an eye for design and a cleanliness of work. He looks at the seams and joints to make sure everything lines up. He looks to see if it's too busy (crowded, with a lot of extraneous things) or too simple. And he can't stress enough the importance of knowing design theories. He suggests that if you can't get to a design school, that you read design magazines. Study what works by looking at what's being made. And above all, keep building.

## Matte Artist

A matte painting is a large painting, usually on glass, that depicts a scene or a location, and a matte artist is someone who paints it.

Matte painting is a highly specialized field, requiring a great knowledge of painting techniques as well as color theory and application. Mattes have to look real for the camera, but not necessarily to the naked eye, so the artist has to be able to create illusions that can blend with live action seamlessly.

Very often, mattes are used to create a background of buildings or scenery into which the live actors will be placed. Mattes can also eliminate things from the shot that shouldn't be seen. For example, in *Raiders of the Lost Ark*, the seaplane Indiana Jones gets on near the beginning of the film was not actually near the ocean. A matte was used to take out the studio surroundings and replace them with rolling water.

## Visual Effects Art Director

Since this is the big time, where people are all working together to make sure everything gets done in time and on budget, someone has to be in charge. Organizing everything, even taking over the design chores every once in awhile (or at least working with the shop people) so that all remains within schedule, is the visual effects art director.

The job of the visual effects art director (which is often synonymous with visual effects supervisor) is much like that of the regular art director (described in Chapter 5), except the visual effects art director works only with the effects of the film. Brent Boates, who started out as a storyboard artist, now supervises all the effects his shop does on any given film he is assigned.

Visual effects art director is not a job you just jump into. Brent went from regular storyboards to effects storyboards, where he spent several years, and then into his current position. During those intervening years, he learned as much as he could about all the different types of special effects and what kind of effect would produce what kind of result. These were things he needed to know to do the storyboards right. In his words, you must "understand the illusion" to ensure its correct outcome.

# Creative Supervisor

One step to the side of a visual effects art director is the creative supervisor. Usually found on television shows rather than on movies, the creative supervisor is the prime administrator for all the effects. He or she will interface between the shop and the producers, from preproduction all the way through the wrap and beyond. David Barrington Holt serves this function for Jim Henson's Creature Shop.

Although David no longer does any designing, he does work with all the show's designers and is a welcome voice, whether for critique or praise. Given the extent of his supervision, David has pretty much given up any hope of life outside the show during the workweek. The main things he brings to the shows he's worked on are diversity and experience. He has done all the jobs he now presides over and knows what he's talking about when he makes a comment or suggestion. His authority and knowledge make things run as smoothly and creatively as possible and ensure the highest production values around.

# For Further Information

Special effects are becoming big business, and a whole breed of educational facilities are cropping up to train people in these specialized arts. These schools range from specific certification schools to full-blown degree programs. In addition to schools, a number of books and magazines are devoted to nothing but special effects in movies and television. These magazines can provide a solid introduction and background for effects work.

## Books

Bizony, Piers. *Digital Domain: The Leading Edge of Visual Effects.* New York: Watson-Guptill Publications.

Perisic, Zoran. *Visual Effects Cinematography.* Burlington, MA: Elsevier Science/Harcourt.

Schechter, Harold. *Film Tricks: Special Effects in the Movies*. New York: Doubleday.

## Magazines

*Cinefantastique*
P.O. Box 270
Oak Park, IL 60303
www.cfq.com

*Cinefex*
P.O. Box 20027
Riverside, CA 92516
www.cinefex.com

*Starlog*
www.starlog.com

## Schools

Jim Henson's Creature Shop, Los Angeles
2821 Burton Avenue
Burbank, CA 91504
www.creaureshop.com

Cinema Make-Up School
3780 Wilshire Boulevard, Third Floor
Los Angeles, CA 90010
www.makeupcollege.com

# CHAPTER NINE

# Editing
## The Cutting Edge

ilm is unique among the visual arts. It has the ability to force your attention to something you may have missed or may not have wanted to see in the first place. It can speed up your adrenaline or slow it down to the point of boredom, all for the desired effect. A director can control things like pacing, rhythm, and mood because film has one device unparalleled in any other art form: a filmmaker has the option of editing.

Some of the best examples of editing can be found by watching MTV. Music videos have created a sense of style and rhythm based almost completely on a unique brand of editing. This fast-paced cutting and splicing has found its way into the mainstream of American movies with directors such as Tarsem Singh and McG, directors of *The Cell* and *Charlie's Angels,* respectively.

However, visuals are not the only things that get edited; the sound and music can have a profound effect on the finished product if done correctly.

Thanks to modern technology, "film" editing is becoming a thing of the past. This isn't to say that film is fading away, but the actual cutting and splicing of little pieces of celluloid is rapidly becoming unnecessary and cost prohibitive. Film editing will always exist. There will always be students and independent filmmakers sitting in dark rooms, running film frame by frame through a flatbed or upright editor. There will continue to be bins filled with cut-up work prints hanging over them, numbered by scene and take numbers, ready to be assembled into a continuous story. What's replacing the standard? Video. Video editing systems that in the mid-1980s were an interesting novelty are now being used with regularity and soon will take over and become the new standard.

In today's electronic world, computers are becoming the cheap and easy path to a finished film. Software applications such as Final Cut Pro, Avid, and Premiere all allow professional-level editing to be done in a home studio. Films such as Steven Soderbergh's *Full Frontal* and Robert Rodriguez's *Spy Kids 2: The Island of Lost Dreams* were both edited on high-end Apple Macintosh computers. Even the most basic computer systems for sale today come packaged standard with video editing software.

But it really hasn't changed anything. The art of editing is still the same. Editors are still using machines as tools; it's just that the machines now are more technologically based.

## Digitizer

So how do you get the images from the camera into the computer? That's where the digitizer comes in. This is a job position that has only been created in the past few years and is rapidly becoming one of the best entry-level jobs going.

What the digitizer does, according to Martin Dunn, is "take all the footage and load it into the hard drive. It's that simple." Not really. Martin also takes an extensive amount of notes, writing down what's on each take, from the scene and take numbers to which character the camera is covering to how long the take lasts and where it comes in the reel. He's also responsible for quality control, making sure every frame makes it through to the digital world.

"This is great training for being an editor," Martin says. "I get to see everything the director shot, and I can mentally piece it together to see how close I come to the final product."

## Assistant Editor

What is an assistant editor? The short answer is that an assistant editor works with the editor to create the finished piece. The long answer is a little more complicated, depending on the size of the production.

On a smaller shoot, the assistant may also digitize and get coffee. On a larger project, the assistant will actually "precut" scenes for the editor, putting together a rough assemblage of shots so the editor has a jumping off point. This doesn't happen in a vacuum, though. The assistant works very closely with the editor to make sure the tone and pace are right for the scene. Often, specific takes will be selected beforehand so everyone knows exactly which material to work with.

Andrew J. Zoeller started out as an assistant and says it is the best possible training. Like most jobs in the industry, you learn by doing. The best place to "do" is with an editor who can watch over you. Andrew developed a teacher/mentor relationship with the editors he worked with, and he'll still call on them to answer questions or give advice. If you work with people who are better at a job than you are, you'll always learn something from them.

## Editor

The editor is the one who actually puts the film together in sequence. It's a long, lonely job with just the editing machine to keep you company. Here's the way it works when film is the primary medium.

When the film comes back from the lab, a positive work print is made from the processed negative of the takes the director wanted printed. These are the takes that are logged in by the assistant and that the editor strings up to get to easily. The editor puts them roughly in sequential order and begins work.

The editor starts assembling the film. He or she takes the master shot of any given scene and intercuts it with an over-the-shoulder shot of one of the actors or maybe a two-shot. Intercutting means just that—actually cutting into the work print and inserting frames from other shots or takes. The editor does this to get a rough idea of how the scene plays, then goes back in and recuts and fine-tunes until satisfied. Each recut may mean adding one frame or taking out two. If the editor doesn't like the changes, those frames have to be put back in. If a scene gets too hacked up, a second or even a third work print is made. When the entire film is done like this, it's called the rough cut. The rough cut is screened by the director, who in all probability has been working closely with the editor anyway, and changes are made. The new version, the one that meets the director's specifications, is called the director's cut. If everybody is happy with it, then the film is released. If not, the film is recut again, this time to producer or studio specifications, and released. This is the final cut.

Nowadays, though, most film is edited electronically, which is how Andrew J. Zoeller does it. So it works a little differently. When the positive takes from the film come in from the lab, they are immediately transferred to an electronic medium—digitized. On a nonlinear system, such as Avid, which Andrew prefers, the takes are put right into a digital storage bank where they can be called up instantly, as with a compact disc. The assistant/digitizer's logging responsibilities then include noting in which storage bank each take is located.

The editing process then proceeds in the same order, but there are no physical frames to deal with. The frames are cut or added with the touch of a button. And with digital editing, as on the Macintosh-based Avid system, Andrew has the option of recutting the same scene many different ways and playing them all back at the same time. This way, he can watch the variations to see which one makes the scene flow the best.

No matter which system you use, though, Andrew says the most important thing is continuity. By developing a coherent story out of the jumble he's given, Andrew creates drama, or comedy, or whatever he's trying to achieve. The best advice he can give to anyone who wants to get into editing is to watch a lot of films. Notice how different editors have a style that works for them. A certain method of cutting will create tension, while the same scene, when edited slightly differently, may be comedic. It's all up to you.

According to Andrew, editing is "fixing the mistakes made in directing," and the more you learn about the process of editing, the fewer of those mistakes you'll make if you ever get your chance behind the camera.

## Negative Cutter

After the editor is done and the final cut of the work print has been approved, the negative has to be cut. From the cut negative, the release prints are made. These are the copies of the film that go out to theaters. Because there is only one negative, you only get one chance, so you can see that it is very important to make sure the negative is cut properly.

How does the negative cutter know where to cut? The cutter gets a list from the editor, then configures the negative to match. This list is called the EDL—the edit decision list. The EDL uses the edge numbers printed on the side of the film (like the numbers on the edge of negatives you get from any standard 35 mm still camera), which correspond to frame numbers. If the editing system is video, the EDL is generated by a computer, which translates a standard form of time code, the SMPTE time code, into edge numbers.

In the room where the cutting is being done, you can have absolutely nothing that may damage the negative. No drinking, smoking, eating, nothing. You need a totally clean environment to work at your best.

The negative cutter also has the responsibility of reprinting any work prints needed by the editor. The cutter sends the negative to the lab with instructions on what to print. There is no room for mistakes in cutting a negative, so if you're a perfectionist with an eye for detailed, methodical work, this is the place for you. The problem, however, lies in the trend to edit on video. For jobs like TV shows or movies for cable, the entire project can be edited on video and, even though shot on film, the negative may never be touched. It's not an easy field to break into, but as long as there are theaters showing films, there will always be a need for negative cutters.

## Colorist

There's an old story about the original "Star Trek" television series that illustrates the job of the colorist. It seems in an early episode, there was an alien woman who had green skin. The makeup department did a wonderful job making her look as if green were her actual skin tone. The scene was shot and sent off to the lab. When the print came back for dailies, the green woman had miraculously become white. Thinking there was something wrong with the way they had shot the scene, the crew went back in and reshot the green woman. Again the film came back from the lab with a white woman. This time the film crew went to the lab to find out what was happening. The technicians at the lab had seen the film come in, seen the green woman, and assumed their equipment had made a mistake. They color-corrected for the green and sent back a woman the right color for a Caucasian human but the wrong color for an alien. Eventually it all got worked out, and the episode became one of the classics from the original series.

Whether that's a true story or not, it tells you what the colorist does. He or she makes sure the color density and shade are consistent from shot to shot.

The colorist works with the director of photography, finding out what the original colors were and what the DP was looking for in terms of color saturation. Then, when the print is being processed, the colorist adjusts the color to match the real-life situation. The colorist also matches for scenes that feature the same setting or costumes, so if an actor is wearing a deep blue jacket in one scene, the same jacket is not a muddy grey in the next.

There are different ways to work with color and become a colorist. When working with film, the easiest way is to find a lab where you can work.

In video, a colorist (also known as a telecine operator) is responsible for matching the color as the film is transferred to video for editing or broadcast purposes.

Either way, you need to have a good eye for color and a fine sense for detail. You can't start as a colorist, but working at any of the film labs in Hollywood (such as FotoKem, Technicolor, Crest National Film Laboratories, or Consolidated Film Industries) or any postproduction house in an entry-level position will get you in the door.

The rest is up to you.

## Dialogue Editor

Every word spoken in a film is considered dialogue. What the dialogue editor does is take all the audiotapes and find the best inflection or clearest reading of each passage, then splice them all together to make the best possible dialogue track. Also under the dialogue editor's supervision is additional dialogue replacement (ADR), or looping, where the actor comes in and rerecords any dialogue not usable from the original location sound. Looping is also a process where other actors not from the original filming come in and record background voices to sonically fill out a scene.

## Supervising Sound Editor

All sound in the film, with the exception of the music, is handled by the supervising sound editor, who oversees everything from ADR to dialogue editing to Foley. The supervising sound editor watches the film and writes cue sheets for the Foley person based on what seems to be needed to add to the dynamics of the film.

At the beginning, the supervising sound editor talks with the director about the sound track. Some directors are in love with sound and want it to be everything it can be and more; others have an indifference and just want it to be there. Either way, the sound editor takes the director's ideas and follows them through all aspects of the sound production, making sure the sound is the perfect complement to what the director has recorded visually.

## Music Editor

Like the dialogue editor, the music editor works on a specific section of the sound track. The music editor works with the composer, taking notes for cues, helping to organize recording sessions, and making sure they run smoothly. Once the recording is done, the music editor actually sits down with the audiotape and cuts it to match the picture. Basically, the music editor is responsible for all the music on the film.

The way to get into it is to start at the bottom. An apprentice is always needed, and if you're willing to work hard and work cheap, you'll get work. From there, you move on to being an assistant, then an editor in your own right. Once you're a music editor, you start the cycle all over when some young kid comes up to you and asks if there's anything he or she can do to help out, and you end up with your very own apprentice.

## For Further Information

Editing is like doing a jigsaw puzzle. Someone (the director) has created a whole picture, then had it cut up and given to you. You've got the box to look at, but you've still got to put it all together so it resembles what the director wanted to begin with. If you can see the whole through the parts, look into these books and the Motion Picture and Videotape Editors Guild for ways to get your hands on the pieces.

## Books

Burder, John, and Gerald Millerson. *16 mm Film Cutting.* Burlington, MA: Elsevier Science/Harcourt.

Kerner, Marvin M. *The Art of the Sound Effects Editor.* Burlington, MA: Elsevier Science/Harcourt.

Murch, Walter. *In the Blink of an Eye.* Los Angeles: Silman-James Press.

Oldham, Gabriella. *First Cut.* Berkeley: University of California Press.

Reisz, Karel, and Gavin Millar. *Technique of Film Editing, 2nd Edition.* Burlington, MA: Elsevier Science/Harcourt.

Rosenblum, Ralph, and Robert Karen. *When the Shooting Stops.* New York: Da Capo Press.

Rubin, Michael. *Nonlinear—a Field Guide to Digital Video and Film Editing, 4th Edition.* Gainesville, FL: Triad Publishing.

Sherman, Eric. *Frame by Frame.* Los Angeles: Acrobat Books.

Wohl, Michael. *Techniques with Final Cut Pro.* Berkeley: Peachpit Press.

## Organization

Motion Picture and Videotape Editors Guild IATSE Local 700
7715 Sunset Boulevard, Suite 200
Hollywood, CA 90046
www.editorsguild.com

# CHAPTER TEN

# On the Fringes

You've made it this far and still haven't found a career that feels just right for you? Not to worry—we still have plenty more things to offer you. You see, making a film is like living in a small town, with the producer as governor. The director then fills in as mayor, and all the other jobs are found around the set. Production assistants become mail carriers, running around delivering script changes and call sheets to everyone who needs them. A film even has its own version of a police force and, sometimes, a fire department.

All films need a wide variety people to handle specific tasks. You can't make a film without someone operating the camera. But depending on the type of film being made, there may be more jobs available than the ones mentioned so far. There are some jobs that are instrumental in getting a film made and shown, but they are not necessarily involved in the actual filmmaking process itself. Even if, while performing these tasks, you find yourself on the set, you still won't be part of the mainstream production crew. A few of those jobs are here, too, as are a few that simply didn't fit elsewhere in this book.

## Film Journalist

If you can write but you're still waiting for your big break as a screenwriter, film journalism may be the place for you. Where else can you spend days on a film location, wandering around as if you're not doing anything, and still get paid for it? Don't think too hard because, unless you're a producer, this is the one and only.

Dan Persons has been doing it for some time. He's a regular contributor to *Cinefantastique* magazine, and he's had the chance to spend time on some of the hottest sets in Hollywood.

For Dan, who graduated from New York University Film School, writing about films came naturally, but he says that having some background knowledge of film technology was a definite plus. "You'd be at a serious disadvantage if you didn't know films aren't shot in sequence."

The way to start a film journalism career is, like film itself, to start with a story. For Dan, it was an introduction to the people responsible for *Toxic Avenger, Part 2.* Just having the meeting and the possibility of an interview was enough to get his foot in the door over at *Cinefantastique.* He told the editor about his connection with the film in the form of a query letter, which is a short pitch of the article idea. The editor liked the idea enough to buy it.

Since Dan started writing for *Cinefantastique,* he hasn't stopped. Rarely does an issue go by without his name appearing somewhere above an article. That first article ran around a thousand words—about four typed, double-spaced pages. Dan recommends a shorter piece when trying to break in, but once established, articles can run anywhere from one thousand to ten thousand words, including sidebars (short companion stories with the main feature).

Now that you've got the assignment, though, how do you go about getting the information to make it all come together? Well, when you're on the set, absorb everything. Usually, a reporter will only get to spend a day, or at most three, on location, so it's best to get as much information as possible. Dan keeps a small notebook handy to jot down details or record conversations among the film's crew. Then he'll get his chance to do interviews. Sometimes, those interviews include the film's stars, but since *Cinefantastique* is geared primarily toward the technical aspects of filmmaking, specifically effects, Dan mainly gets to interview the craftspeople about what they do. He's interviewed directors, writers, production designers, and effects people on films ranging from *Toxic*

*Avenger, Part 2* to hits like *The Silence of the Lambs* to films that may go straight to video, such as *Robocop 3*. It was in these interviews that Dan's film background helped out. By knowing what these people did on the job, he was able to ask them questions that focused on their abilities and their special contributions to the production.

The great thing about writing about films is that you never have to lose the sense of wonder and fascination that first brought you to the field because there's always something new going on, and you're always a part of it.

## Animal Trainer

Are you good with animals? Have you been able to teach the family dog to sit or stay or fetch? Good. Now it's time to move on to the next step: teaching the family mountain lion to attack and kill an actor on cue. Well, actually to make it look as if the lion is attacking and killing the actor without harming either. That's the job of an animal trainer.

Animal training is a highly specialized field. Not only do you have to know how to talk to the animals, but you have to know how to talk to a lot of different animals. Once you're talking, though, it's not over. You have to be able to teach whatever animal you're working with the tricks, or behaviors, requested by the director or script.

If the script calls for our friendly neighborhood mountain lion to defend the human family he's adopted, then that's just what the lion has to do. The director may want the lion to jump down on the bad guys from the roof of the family's house, then run around and corner the bad guy against the wall, but not actually attack until the bad guy makes a run for it. The trainer may spend weeks walking the animal through the scene, acclimating it to what it is supposed to do. Once the animal knows its routine, then the actor is brought in to rehearse the scene. Even though these animals, especially the big cats, seem friendly and tame, they are still wild, and accidents have been known to happen. The trainer, who knows the animal better than anyone, is on the set whenever the animal is and is the one who walks the actor through the scene with the animal. As long as there are no surprises to the animal, everything should go off exactly as planned.

It takes years to be a trainer. There are some schools throughout the country that offer specialized courses in animal care and training, but one of the most effective ways to discover if you're cut out for the field is to work directly with the animals. In Hollywood and its outlying areas, there are several animal ranches that provide critters for all types of film and television work. The trainers here are happy to answer questions from people who love and respect animals as much as they do.

## Animal Wrangler

Don't confuse animal wrangler with animal trainer. They are not necessarily the same thing. True, you should have experience with whatever type of animal you're wrangling, but you're not really training them. It's more of an entry level to the world of animal training.

The main job of an animal wrangler, also called animal handler, is to keep a group of animals in line and doing what they are supposed to be doing. In *Raiders of the Lost Ark*, there was a snake wrangler. *Batman Returns* had a penguin wrangler. *Eight Legged Freaks* had a spider wrangler. In each case, the wrangler had to make sure the animals stayed within the shot. If, during the tomb sequence of *Raiders of the Lost Ark*, one of the snakes happened to slither away between takes, the wrangler had to put it back.

A wrangler or handler is also responsible for individual animals, such as horses. The handler should be able to instruct the actor in the proper handling of the creature while the cameras are rolling. If the actor has to ride the horse, then the handler must be able to give the actor at least enough instruction to make it look as if the actor actually knows how to ride.

# Dance Choreographer

There are a couple of different types of choreography. The first is dance. A dance choreographer designs the movement of any dancing in the film. Even if the film isn't a musical, there may be a scene where the two leads are waltzing across the roof during a tender romantic moment. This scene needs a choreographer.

Most dance choreographers are well versed in a variety of styles of dance styles. A choreographer works up through the ranks, usually starting as a dancer, to get to the position of controlling the action.

The dance choreographer has to know more than just dance, however. Like the rest of the crew, the choreographer needs to understand mood and period. If the film is a musical taking place in the 1960s, then the dance style needs to reflect it. The style is also dictated by social class and geographical location. Look at the difference in the dancing on the turn-of-the-century Parisian set *Moulin Rouge* compared to the modern-day high school comedy *She's All That*. With the growing awareness of world beat and global influences, dance forms are constantly changing, and the choreographer needs to keep up with the changes.

# Fight Choreographer

The second type of choreography is fight, or combat, choreography. Any time two characters are fighting hand to hand or with handheld weapons such as swords or knives, then the fight has to be choreographed. Otherwise, if the actors try to set up the fight themselves, there's a good chance one or both of them will get hurt. Ask Cynthia McArthur; her job is to make sure that doesn't happen.

Just as a dance choreographer designs movements, Cynthia designs fights. She has to know what works and what doesn't. "Realistic fights don't shoot well," she says. "Historically accurate fights weren't pretty and never lasted more than a few seconds—

boring." Her main concern, from the very beginning, is the safety of the actors, especially when they're using her favorite form of combat, fencing. Even swords that have blunted tips and dulled edges can still, as your mother was fond of saying, poke your eye out. With that in mind, Cynthia always starts out by blocking the fight on paper. This gives her a rough idea of where the action is going to take place and where on the set the actors will be. The paper fight will then be shown to the director, and adjustments will be made. Once the paper fight is given a tentative final approval, physical blocking will start.

At this point in the process, several other elements come into play. Depending on how the director is going to shoot the fight, Cynthia will adapt her choreography. If the fight is between two principal actors, and both of their faces will be seen, then Cynthia has to teach both of them the complete routine. This includes showing each of them the correct moves and the order in which they'll come in the fight. All of this is done in extremely slow motion, over and over again, until the actors can perform the moves almost without thinking about them. Only then does the tempo pick up, a little bit at a time, until they are up to performance speed.

If both principals aren't shown all the time or the fight is between the star and a minor player, then Cynthia often doubles for the actor fighting the star. Cynthia, or her husband Jeff, who is also a fight choreographer, sometimes even gets the chance to be in the film as the nameless fencer fighting the hero. In such cases, the fights can become a little more complex because at least one of the fighters is a professional. However, Cynthia is quick to point out that the most successful fights are incredibly simple: "If it's done right, the fight will look complex but still be simple enough to give the performer time to act."

Cynthia didn't come to this green. This is a person who has a full suit of armor in her living room. She has a thorough knowledge of competition fencing and hangs out with people who know metal and build swords. She can tell you, according to time period, if you should cut and parry or hack and slash. She also has a fair grasp on several of the hand-to-hand martial arts, so she can choreograph those as well.

As for getting into the field, Cynthia says fighting is the only way to go. Learn as many styles as you can and practice, practice, practice. Videotape yourself to learn what looks good; even volunteer to work with local theater groups. Stage combat is a little easier than film fighting because you don't have as many angles to deal with. Cynthia says the stage is the best place to learn and a great place to build your resume. Finally, watch as many swashbuckler films as you can get your hands on. Nobody does it like Errol Flynn, but more recent hits such as *The Matrix* and *Crouching Tiger, Hidden Dragon* show exactly where technology can take the art of the fight.

. . . . . . . . . . . . . . . . .

# Stand-In

You may think a stand-in is just somebody who stands on a mark while the actor lounges around and waits for the cameras to roll. Robert Bennett says that's what he thought it was when he first started, but the job of stand-in is so much more than that. Robert has served as a double for some of the biggest names in Hollywood. In film, Robert has stood in for Michael J. Fox and Joe Pesci. In fact, Fox specifically requested Robert for most of his projects.

For a feature film, Robert is almost always on the set. He is there taking notes while the actor he's standing in for goes through the blocking of the scene. Once the blocking is completed, the actor is no longer required, so Robert steps in and literally walks through the role. He helps the gaffers and the chief lighting technician eliminate shadows and make sure the lighting is correct. He pays attention while the lights are being set up, and he knows, according to the blocking, whether his actor will be directly in the light or just to one side.

Robert also checks the set for safety features. If something looks dangerous, he tells the director about it. Usually, this results in whatever it is being taken care of long before the actor ever sees it. Robert has saved productions time and money by being highly observant. But his job doesn't end when the actor is done for the day. As long as the actor will be working again, Robert will run lines and blocking with him, helping him to prepare for his time in front of the camera.

On a television show filmed with a studio audience, Robert's job is a little different. On "Full House," for example, Robert may stand in for several different actors, depending on things such as prior engagements or union rules. In these situations, Robert actually performs the blocking for the actor, who may be doing a second show or, because he is under eighteen, is not able to work full days. When the actor does have time to be on the set, Robert teaches him the blocking. The end result is that the actor gets the time needed to work on performance while the crew gets the time to finish sets and hang lights with someone there to be the actor's representative—a great deal for all involved.

The best thing of all for Robert is that his close contact with stars and the way the films are made has put him into a position where he is able to leap into writing and directing. It's a big leap, but being a stand-in has narrowed the gap a bit.

## Agent

If you ask anyone starting out in the industry what the most powerful position is, you'd probably be surprised by the answer. It's not an actor, not a director or producer, not even the head of a major studio. The most powerful people in Hollywood? Agents.

Why is an agent the most powerful person in Hollywood? Because an agent has control over what the actors, directors, and producers do. The agent can recommend deals, put together packages, and create superstar bundles. Primarily, though, the agent's responsibility is to get the client work.

Agents represent mostly above-the-line talent. This means that if you want to deal with a writer, actor, director, and sometimes a producer, you have to go through that person's agent. The agent handles all preliminary correspondence, acting as an intermediary for the client. Once the deal is ready to happen, the agent controls all negotiations, trying to get the client the most money and benefits possible. The agent also contracts for things like movie poster details, boxes around the clients' names or how big those names are and where they should appear on the poster. If an actor's name appears on the poster in large letters above the title of the film, the agent contracted for it to be that way. It wasn't an accident or the production company being nice.

It is in the agent's best interest to get as much as possible for the client because that's how the agent gets paid. Agents work strictly on commission, usually 10 to 15 percent of the client's earnings. Unless you happen to represent the next Tom Cruise as your first client, it will take years of hard work before you can even think of becoming a top agent. Almost all agents today have advanced degrees, either in business or in law, and they all started out as assistants or even lower. It's rumored that there was a time when the entire mail room staff at the William Morris Agency, one of the top five agencies in Hollywood, held law degrees. You have to start out at the bottom and work your way up. That's the way it's done in the world of artist representation.

Once you make it to agent, though, you can't rest. You are constantly on the phone trying to make deals or stir up interest in your client. You'll always be reading scripts, either by your writing clients or by producers who want your actors to star in their films. Two or three lunch meetings a day, and on weekends you're attending screenings of somebody's latest film. It's a lot of hard work, but if you can bring a project to life, it is worth it. Then you are the magician.

## Film Commissioner

Who is the filmmaker's best friend? If you're shooting on a location in another state or even in a different part of your own, your best friend is probably going to be the film commissioner for the area. The film commissioner is the one who is going to help you set your locations, make sure you have the necessary permits, and generally try to ensure your happiness on location.

You see, the film commissioner is almost like a sales representative for the city or state. The commissioner wants you to come in and spend your production dollars, and with the money a film can generate, that can be quite a bit. In Nevada, for instance, the fiscal year of 2001–2002 brought in an estimated $154 million. Considering that the film commission responsible spent less than half a million to get it, that's a lot of profit.

In Nevada, the film office director is Charlie Geocaris, and it's his office Steven Soderbergh went through to get permission to film *Ocean's 11* on the Las Vegas city streets.

For all film commissions, though, the job starts with the script, which is broken down by the commission's staff. The staff members review all the different locations the script requires and determine which ones they can provide.

But the greatest responsibility of a film commissioner is to balance what the client (the production company) needs with what the community will tolerate. You can't have huge explosions on a residential street at three o'clock in the morning without causing some complaints. And in Las Vegas, where 70 percent of Nevada filming is done, the balance is especially important. The office of the film commission works as a liaison with the hotels and resorts of the city to accommodate film crews whenever possible.

Once balance is achieved, the next obstacle is to try to get more work for your state. In Nevada, the lights of Vegas are great for certain scenes, but a short drive out of town and you're in the middle of the desert, or a few hours north and you find yourself in snow-covered mountains. For example, the film *Misery*, which was set in Colorado, was shot almost entirely in Nevada.

When all the schedules are set, the film office handles day-to-day problems as they occur and even acts as a disinterested third party for union negotiations.

It's not a very glamorous job. You won't get wined and dined, and the only time you visit the set is to handle complications. But if you have a thorough knowledge of film and TV, and if you want to bring some of it to your community, apply at your local film commissioner's office.

## On-Set Medical Crew Member

When you have a film that relies heavily on stunts, or there are a lot of explosions, there is the chance people might get hurt. No matter how carefully things are planned, accidents happen. The best thing to do, for added protection, is to make sure there are trained medical people on the set, standing by with an ambulance to care for anyone hurt whenever these situations arise.

The on-set medical crew is hired on a day-to-day basis and is made up of emergency medical technicians (EMTs) and paramedics, usually employed by an ambulance company. This is not really a film industry job, but if you have medical training and a production comes to town, you just might find yourself on the set.

## Caterer

About five or six hours after the crew's call time, people are going to be hungry. Not for a light snack—that's what craft services is for. The film folks have been working hard, using up a lot of calories, and they are going to want a meal. Who are you going to call? The caterers.

Catering is very important to a film set. A good caterer can get your crew to do back flips for you. Caterers arrive a bit before lunchtime and set up tables, almost like a mock dining room, for the crew. This dining room is portable, so the caterers talk to the assistant director to find a bit of unused location where they can set up. If it's a cold day, and the tables are outside, the caterers set up portable heaters to keep everybody comfortable. Food is served buffet style, with plenty for everyone. A production does not want the crew going hungry.

To get into the catering field, it's best to love food and start with an existing company. If you don't have any kitchen experience, you'll start out serving or driving, but it's easy to work your way up until you can cook your heart out.

# Craft Services Representative

The craft services representative is often a very popular person on the set. The caterers show up once, maybe twice, a day, so what do you do if you're hungry and they are not around? After all, you're out there working hard on the set, using energy. You need your nourishment.

Visit the craft services table. The craft services people make sure you're taken care of for all those between-meal snacks. When you get there in the morning, they have a table set up, stocked with coffee and doughnuts to get you going. Throughout the day, they have a variety of snacks and beverages there for you to come by and grab while you're working.

The best craft services people talk to all the crew members as they come by, asking them what they like and don't like. Some of the more experienced crew will tell the craft services people what they want right away.

By the second or third day of the shoot, craft services will have things up and running with individual tastes in mind. The vegetarians will have chilled celery and natural fruit juices, while the sugar addicts will find a supply of candy bars and cola.

Working craft services means you have to get up early and do your shopping before you get to the set. If the location is standing, then you can leave things set up from day to day, but if the production moves, so do you. Knowing how to brew an excellent cup of coffee can go a long way in getting you hired for this position.

# Studio Teacher

We've all seen those cute, adorable children in movies such as Steven Spielberg's *E.T., the Extra-Terrestrial* and *The Lost World: Jurassic Park 2*. What were they doing making a movie when they should have been in school? Well, Adria Later was on both those sets as a studio teacher, and she can verify that not only were those kids in school, but they all completed their assignments on time.

Adria had to be there. It's required by California state law to have a certified studio teacher on the set to administer to the needs of young people between the ages of six and eighteen. Adria fit the bill. She is not only a studio teacher, but she also holds the titles of welfare worker and baby wrangler and, as such, is responsible for the schooling and well-being of all the children in her care on the set. On *Hook*, Adria was the chief studio teacher and had five other teachers working under her; she was kind of like a studio principal.

All studio teachers are also welfare workers. To be certified as a studio teacher in California (other states don't have anything similar), Adria had to be state credentialed as both an elementary and secondary instructor. Then she had to pass a test on the labor laws of the industry, which are quite stringent. As soon as those things were done, Adria received her "green card," which showed she was a certified teacher. That card is mandatory if you want to work in California or anywhere in the world for a production company based in California.

The test for your green card asks questions about how long children of different ages can stay on the set, how much schooling they need each day, and how long their breaks should be.

The job of a studio teacher is not necessarily traditional. Frequently, the student arrives on set with assignments and books from the regular school classroom, and the studio teacher is there to help out, answer questions, and teach the assignments given by the regular teacher. Adria is often in contact with her student's school, faxing homework to the teacher on a daily basis, so that when finished on the film project, the student will be at the same place as the other classmates at school. Since most of the regular performers are from Los Angeles, where shows are usually taped, they can attend their own school a minimum of once a week (Friday) or in the mornings before coming to work. In this case, the students bring homework with them, and Adria is there to help out when things get tough.

## Stunt Performer

The most dangerous job you can have on any film production is doing stunts. A stunt is any physical activity that might injure the actor, whether or not the actor performs it. There are many different types of stunts requiring different types of skills and training. All of them require that the stunt performer be in good, if not great, physical condition. All stunt people must be members of the Screen Actors Guild.

Generally, a film uses a different stunt performer for each kind of stunt. Some of the stunts you'll find on an average action-adventure film include:

Aerial acrobatics
Fights
High falls
Precision driving
Vehicle crashes

Of these stunts, the ones that require the most training and skill are the ones involving vehicles. In any of the others, you're dealing with a choreographed event and just the stunt performers, which isn't to say these are not dangerous—they are. Do not jump off your roof in an attempt to train for a career in stunts. Everyone you see performing a stunt in front of the camera has had years of training, and the entire event has been worked out with maximum safety in mind. The thing that makes vehicle crashes, and especially precision driving, particularly dangerous is that the driver is dealing with a machine that, if things go horribly wrong, may not react the way it's supposed to.

Because of this, Georgia Durante won't let any of her drivers out without coming to her private monthly safety classes. Georgia is a stunt driver with, and owner/teacher/choreographer of, Performance Two, one of Hollywood's top-three precision driving teams. For her and her team, safety is the most important thing about driving.

Precision driving, as you may guess, is involved in any car or motorcycle chases you see on screen. Weaving in and out of traffic, power skids, bootlegger reverses, ramp jumps—that's all precision stuff. But so is all the driving you see on television car commercials, such as the ones where there is a line of twelve or fifteen cars, and they're all within two inches of each other's bumpers. "You've got to train your mind to think of the driver in front of you and the driver behind you," Georgia says. "And get rid of any ego you may have. Ego gets in the way of driving."

Don't expect to come out to Los Angeles and join a driving team right away. Precision driving is probably the toughest part of the industry to break into. Even if you're the best driver in the world, you're still going to work hard for five or more years before you can start making a living at it. All directors want to work with drivers they trust, and that doesn't come easily. In fact, if you're never driven professionally before, Georgia insists you get some training before coming out and trying to make it a career.

Before training, you should ask yourself it it's something you really want to do. Georgia says she can tell right away if someone has what it takes to be a driver. The first thing you need is a good feel for the car, and you'll know if you have it. The second thing you need is respect for the car. You also need to have confidence in yourself. If you're over- or underconfident, you could get yourself or someone else seriously hurt or killed. If you have what it takes, take classes. There are several tracks throughout the country that offer high-performance driving instruction, the best being Bob Bondurant's schools in Arizona. Once you've graduated from a school, find someone in the profession to take you under a wing, teach you, help you.

Once you do get onto a team, however, the places you can go are limitless. You can stick with commercial precision driving or move up to film and television, doing high-visibility stunts like ramp jumps. Georgia (who has been doing this for more than twelve years) and her team can design a jump anywhere, using their own ramp or one built on location, and land a car within six inches of where they said they would. That is definitely precise.

## Technical Advisor

Being a technical advisor is one job you don't have to train for years to do. The only requirement is that you know something nobody else does, or at least how to communicate it.

Directors use technical advisors when they're dealing with a subject matter they know little about but it is essential that the actors behave as if they have been doing it for years. In films such as *Saving Private Ryan* or TV shows such as "Band of Brothers," the technical advisor was Captain Dale Dye, who could instruct the actors to help them seem authentic—teach them the specialized language and period equipment used by the soldiers.

Technical advisors show up all over the place. Films involving the police have police technical advisors; films taking place in fourteenth-century England have technical advisors who are experts in medieval England.

So, no matter what you know, if you can show others how to look as if they know all about it as well, you have the makings of a technical advisor.

........................

# Film Teacher

You've been reading about all the different and varied jobs there are for you within the film industry. The lucky few will be able to come out to Hollywood and walk right into a job doing something, if not in the actual field, at least related. But even these fortunate job seekers probably had some kind of experience before they hit the California pavement. Odds are, they got that experience in one of two places: either they worked on some kind of production in their hometowns, or, the more likely of the two, they went to film school.

Okay, so film school may be a good idea, but what do we know about the instructors who are teaching you about the industry you love and want to make into a career? Well, we know Holly Willis, a film teacher at the prestigious University of Southern California. Actually, what Holly does is not called teaching at most major colleges and universities. At USC, she's considered a teacher's assistant, which shows how things differ from college to college. Holly's discussion group includes just a fraction of the more than seven hundred students the teacher speaks to in each class. She is responsible for interpreting the lectures of the teacher, handing out and grading assignments, and generally making sure the students understand the subject.

Each film school has its own setup and emphasis of study. Of all the major film schools, there are generally two directions any film program will take. You will leave school with a degree in either film production or film theory.

## Film Production Teacher

Production classes are where the students learn all aspects of production. Pretty much everything covered in this book is something taught in production. As a production student, you will make from one to more than a dozen short films, from short experimental pieces on digital; to video; to silent, three-minute,

Super 8 mm sequences; to a full-blown, sound-synchronized, twenty-five-minute, 16 mm color featurette. On each of these films, you will learn a different job and handle numerous tasks. Production classes are a great training ground for you to get your feet wet and figure out what you like best.

Production instructors are there to guide you through the various steps it's going to take you to get to the finished film. If you're not sure whether to use a five or ten kilowatt, the instructor is the one to ask. As a film instructor, you have to know what you're talking about. That's why the schools are filled with teachers who have been making movies for years and have now decided to pass along their practical knowledge. The new breed of production teachers have some experience going into the job and are ready to share.

## Film Theory Teacher

If the hands-on approach isn't your bag, then what you're looking for may be film theory or critical studies. This is where the aesthetics of filmmaking come into play. Instead of learning what a grip does, you'll learn how and why a Dutch angle is used to elicit a certain emotional response by studying how it has been used in the past by other directors.

What Holly Willis covers in her USC discussion groups is the language of film. She is able to talk about specific film genres or directors or specific films and how they affect the rest of cinema as a whole.

In theory programs, you get a broader view of the world. Theory incorporates ideas as diverse as poststructuralism, psychoanalysis, feminism, Marxism, and issues surrounding race. All these varied philosophies wormed their way into all the other forms of art and into film. Around 1968, it was finally realized that the flickering images of celluloid could be used to convey powerful messages, and that is what studying film theory teaches: how to interpret or even harness those messages for your own purposes. As a teacher of theory, Holly is versed in the history of all film and the watershed moments that led to the present state of the industry, both mainstream and underground.

Since theory is so heavily based on academic learning, almost all critical studies instructors have master's degrees, and many have doctorates, all in the aspect of film theory they teach.

## For Further Information

The following books provide insight into some of the fringe jobs you'll find in the film world.

Blum, Laurie. *Free Money for People in the Arts.* New York: Macmillan Publishing.

Small, Edgar. *From Actor to Agent.* Hollywood: Samuel French Publishing.

Turner, Cherie. *Stunt Performers: Life Before the Camera.* New York: Rosen Publishing Group.

Wiener, David J. *Burns, Falls and Crashes: Interviews with Movie Stunt Performers.* Jefferson, NC: McFarland and Company, Inc., Publishers.

# Glossary

F ilm, like most industries, has a language all its own. This brief glossary includes terms you're likely to hear around a film set or in a production office. These aren't all of them, and many change from set to set, but this should give you enough information to understand what everyone is talking about.

**77 or Super 77**  3M brand spray adhesive.

**Above-the-line talent**  The top creative talent: actors, writers, directors, and producers.

**AC**  Assistant camera operator.

**ACE**  American Cinematic Editors (professional editors' association).

**AD**  Assistant director.

**ADR**  Additional dialogue replacement, a process whereby an actor's voice is manipulated to match the visual of the lips moving.

**AFTRA**  American Federation of Television and Radio Artists.

**Apple box**  A small wooden box about the size of an old apple crate, used for just about anything from stepladders to stools to bases for props. They come in four sizes: full, half, quarter, and eighth (pancakes).

**Arri**  Company that makes the Arriflex Camera System.

**ASC**  American Society of Cinematographers.

**Audition**  The process of trying an actor out for a particular role.

**Barn doors**   Four hinged flaps placed in front of the light, used to direct it or cut it off from certain areas.

**Below-the-line talent**   The production professionals and crew members who make a film happen—everyone except the actors, screenwriters, producers, and directors.

**BG**   Background; also animators who specialize in drawing backgrounds.

**B-roll**   Behind-the-scenes footage of the working set. Usually sent out as part of an electronic press kit (see *EPK*).

**BSC**   British Society of Cinematographers.

**C-47s**   Clothes pins.

**Call sheet**   A listing of all the shots to be done during the day. It includes which actors, props, and costumes are needed as well as any special requirements, such as effects or explosions. It is distributed the day before and lists individual and department call times (the time you must be on set).

**CGI**   Computer-generated images.

**Cheaters**   Cue cards.

**Check the gates**   Checking the camera's aperture for dust or hair to ensure a clean shot.

**Clapboard**   A small slate with black-and-white sticks at the top, used to signal the beginning or end of a take.

**Claymation**   Stop-motion animation using posable clay figures.

**Color sheets**   New script pages. After the first draft, which is white, every time a scene is rewritten, it is given a new color. This is where you get pages in pink, blue, green, and so forth.

**Cookie cutter**   See *Gobo*.

**Copies provided**   Your payment, usually on student productions, is a copy of the finished product.

**Crate**   See *Apple box*.

**Credits**   The lists at the front (beginning) and tail (end) of the film naming the people involved with the film and what jobs they did. Also, all the jobs you've done in the past.

**CSA**   Casting Society of America.

**Cue cards**   Cards with dialogue written on them, placed out of camera view but where the actor can see them.

**Cut**   A command issued by the director to tell the camera, sound, and action to stop.

**Dailies**   The footage shot the day before, shown to the director, usually without sound sweetening or color correction.

**Deal memo**   The contract you sign when you're hired, which states your title and salary.

**Deferred pay**   Instead of being paid up front, you get paid only if the film makes money.

**DGA**   Directors Guild of America.

**Digitizing**   The process of inputting footage into a computer editing or effects system.

**DP**   Director of photography. Known as a DOP in England.

**DV**   Digital video.

**DVE**   Digital video effect.

**EDL**   Edit decision list. A list of film frame numbers given to the negative cutter by the editor or to an online editor from an offline system.

**EPK**   Electronic press kit. Information sent on videotape to a visual media outlet (a TV show) for use when putting together a story.

**Equity**   Actors' Equity Association, the union for stage actors.

**Flat**   A thin wall used to represent an actual wall. For film, flats are usually made of quarter-inch plywood sheets. In the theater, they are made of half-inch planks covered by muslin.

**Foley stage**   A large, soundproof room designed to re-create real-world sounds.

**FPS**   Frames per second.

**Gaffer**   Chief lighting technician.

**Gel**   A thin piece of colored plastic that can change the color of the light.

**Gobo**   A cutout shape placed in front of a light that causes the light to project the shape. In theater, gobos are used to represent things like trees or clouds; in film, they also help break up the light.

**Grip**   A person who moves and helps set up equipment on the set.

**Grip tape**   A strong, heavy-duty tape, usually fibrous, used to hold things together on a set.

**Hollywood Blu-Book**   A directory listing the various production people and services in the Los Angeles area published by the Hollywood Reporter. See also *Hollywood creative directories* and *LA 411.*

**Hollywood creative directories**   A series of books listing names, credits, and contact information for writers, directors, producers, cinematographers, and below-the-line talent. See also *Hollywood Blu-Book* and *LA 411.*

**Hot head**   A camera and mount combination that can rotate in a complete circle, 360 degrees.

**Hot set**   A set that is still being used, so nothing is to be touched. Usually it's taped off if a day ended without everything on it being shot.

**IATSE**   International Alliance of Theatrical and Stage Employees, the alliance of unions that comprises most of the Hollywood below-the-line unions.

**In the can**   Finished product.

**Insert**   A close-up of an item added in during editing. Can be filmed away from the main action on a specialized "insert stage."

**Intern**   Person (usually student) who works without pay in a chosen job. Working for the experience usually leads to a paying job.

**Ivy**   A trendy Los Angeles restaurant where famous people eat.

**Junket**   A press event where the media are invited to meet the stars and above-the-line talent for a film. Used for promotional purposes.

**Key**   The head of a particular section or department.

**LA 411**   A directory listing the various production people and services in the Los Angeles area published by *Variety*. See also *Hollywood Blu-Book* and *Hollywood creative directories*.

**Lamp**   Lightbulb.

**Makita**   A tool company that makes cordless power tools, primarily a reversible drill that is indispensable on a set where things are constantly being screwed and unscrewed.

**Masking**   Hiding something from the camera's view.

**MOS**   A sound term meaning to shoot picture without corresponding audio. Popular myth says the initials stand for either "Mit Out Sound," attributed to a German director, or "Minus Optical Sound."

**Nagra**   A type of location audio recorder popular on feature films.

**NTSC**   American video standard, shoots at thirty frames per second.

**One sheet**   The standard size of a movie poster in a theater lobby.

**PA**   Production assistant.

**PAL**   European video standard, shoots at twenty-five frames per second.

**Panavision**   Company that makes the Panaflex camera system.

**Pancake**   Flat apple box.

**Panning**   A side-to-side movement of a camera, or writing a bad review of a film.

**Post**   Postproduction.

**PR**   Public relations or publicity.

**Principal photography**   The bulk of the filming with the main actors present.

**Reel**   A roll of film or a video resume of clips of your work.

**Reset**   Putting the set back together for another take. This involves making everything the way it was before the take started. Also known as putting things "back to one."

**Resume**   A written list of your credits.

**Room tone**   The ambient noise in any location, recorded by the sound mixer.

**Rushes**   See *Dailies*.

**SAE**   Self-addressed envelope.

**SAG**   Screen Actors Guild.

**Sandbags**   Bags filled with sand used to weigh things down.

**SASE**   Self-addressed, stamped envelope.

**Save the light**   Turn the light off to extend the life of the lamp.

**Screen test**   Auditioning an actor on camera to see how well he or she photographs.

**Screening**   A viewing of the final film for the cast and crew.

**Scrim**   A piece of fabric that lets light pass through it from one side and is used to cause a varying amount of diffusion.

**SECAM**   Asian video standard, shoots at twenty-eight frames per second.

**Second unit**   A backup team that films inserts and any specialized shots, such as aerial photography, establishing shots, or stunts.

**Servility**   A three-prong plug with the ground removed or broken off.

**Sides**   The script pages for a particular scene (rather than the whole script) given to an actor to rehearse for a scene or audition.

**Slate**   See *Clapboard*.

**SMPTE**   A standard form of time code.

**Spec**   Speculation, doing something on your own in the hopes someone will eventually pay you for it. Most common among writers who write spec scripts.

**Speed**   When said by the sound mixer, this term means the audiotape has synchronized with the camera and is now ready to record.

**Spike mark**   A mark made on the floor, usually with tape, to signify where something is supposed to be. It could be for the actor as a place to stand, where a set piece needs to be returned to during a reset, or to tell the dolly where to stop. To place one, the request "spike this" is usually given.

**Squibs**   Miniature explosives used in effects. Usually, they are attached to an actor's body to simulate bullet hits.

**Standee**   A large promotional display placed in the lobby of a theater.

**Steadicam**   A device used to make camera movements extremely fluid.

**Sticks**   Tripod or clapboard.

**Stinger**   Extension cord.

**Stop motion**   Animation technique in which the animator poses a creature, shoots a single frame of film, moves the creature slightly, shoots another frame, and so on to create an illusion of fluid movement in the finished film.

**Strip board**   Little strips the assistant director uses to organize the shooting schedule. Each strip has one scene and is designed to be rearranged easily.

**Sweetening**   Tightening up the sound (and video) in post-production to get rid of hiss or any other unnecessary glitches. To make the sound and images all match.

**Take**   Each time the camera rolls film for a particular scene.

**Three-camera shoot**   A television show shot with three cameras all going at the same time. The technique was created for the "I Love Lucy" show. Also four-camera shoot.

**Tilting**   An up-and-down movement of the camera.

**Time code**   A referencing system that ensures that all components are running at the same speed and match exactly frame by frame.

**Trailer**   The preview of coming attractions (new films) seen before the feature presentation at the theater.

**Walkaround**   A self-contained costume suit worn by a person playing a cartoon character or mascot.

**WGA**   Writers Guild of America.

**Working**   If a prop, costume, or set is being used that day, it's considered working.

**Wrap**   With one exception, this is yelled by the assistant director to signify the end of the day. When said by the director, "wrap" signifies the end of production.

**Wrap beer**   Alcohol broken out at the end of the shooting day or week.

**Wrap party**   A party held at the end of production.

# About the Author

••••••••••••••••••••••••••••••••••••••••••••••••••••••••••••

Jaq Greenspon splits his time among homes in Santa Monica, Las Vegas, London, and Long Itchington (in the United Kingdom). When not making movies of his own, Jaq enjoys watching other people's efforts. He has written for several TV series including "Star Trek: The Next Generation" and "The New Adventures of Robin Hood." In print, Jaq has written two books for the Careers for You series and hundreds of articles about filmmaking and motorcycles. His first novel, a murder mystery set in Venice, California, is making the rounds in New York, looking for the right publisher. Currently, he is hard at work on his second novel, this one set against the background of professional hockey.